"HE KILLED OUR JANNY": A Family's Search for the Truth

SHERRIE LUEDER

The names of some individuals in this book have been changed. Such names are indicated by an asterisk (*) the first time each appears in the book.

ISBN-13: 978-1466283282
ISBN-10: 1466283289

DEDICATION

In Loving Memory of
Janyce Hansen
Beloved daughter, sister, mother and grandmother

"Her beauty made the dim world brighter"

ACKNOWLEDGEMENTS

Thank you to John and Jill for courageously sharing your memories and granting me the opportunity to write your story.

Thank you to my sister, Kim, who has worked with me on the book from start to finish. Thank you for your extensive research in uncovering the facts and the many interviews you conducted.

Thank you to our family and friends for your helpful suggestions. Thank you for your love and support when many times we would decline an invitation by replying "sorry we have to work on the book".

Thank you to Cindy Scott, Eric Soltz, and Janny's other close friends for bringing truth to our story.

Thank you to the authorities and experts within the following departments who helped our own investigation by answering questions and offering advice--Aurora Police Department, Attorney General's Office, District Attorney's Office, F.B.I. and the Arapahoe County Coroner's Office.

Thank you to the select few, Katrina Laura Klein Masterson (United States Federal Government/Justice Department), George McGoff (retired CSI Agent), Victoria Lovato (former Detective), Susan Murphy-Milano, Dennis Griffin, Vito Collucci, Jr., and Thomas Shamshank (Crime Wire Team) who have helped open new avenues to explore, and for their continued support in our quest for the truth.

Thank you to Bonnie Hearn Hill, our friend and editor, for your expertise in editing and polishing our manuscript.

For us who believe—thank you fate.

PREFACE

This is a true story based on the recollections of Janyce Hansen's children, John Hansen and Jill Hansen Smith, further substantiated by interviews, police reports and various state, city and county officials within the jurisdiction of Arapahoe County and the State of Colorado.

This book is an amazing story of a fight for survival and quest for justice. As Janny's mother said over and over from the beginning "he killed our Janny". Now, through our own research and investigation, we have been told by several law enforcement officers and experts that they too believe Richard could have killed Janny, as the family believes.

I am passionate about this project, not only as the author, but because I have a personal connection with the family. I have worked hand in hand with John, Jill and Kim for the past two years to make this book a reality. The courage John and Jill have shown through reliving the past is remarkable. In fact, at one point Jill slipped into a coma and nearly died. I felt their pain and cried with them as they told heart wrenching stories of suffering and abuse at the hands of Richard. I also felt their love when remembering their mother.

Janny was a beautiful young woman who most certainly loved her family and life more than death.

ONE

The residents living along Cedar Avenue felt secure going to sleep at night with their windows open when the weather permitted. After all, they lived in a fairly newly developed, upper-class neighborhood in Aurora, Colorado. Beautiful homes lined either side of the avenue, with Aurora Hills Golf Course backing to the houses on the north side of the street.

On the evening of Thursday, September 20, 1984, Karen Hudson* went to sleep with her bedroom window open. Sometime later, she was awakened by shouting outside. She lay in bed for a few seconds and then got up to investigate. *Now what*, she thought. Most likely the Hansens. Party central over there. Never a dull moment living across the street from them. Every time you turned around, something was going on. If it wasn't the slutty-looking women or the shady characters coming and going at all hours, then it was the cops. She hadn't really gotten to know her neighbors yet, and she didn't want to. The lady seemed nice enough. She would smile and wave when they passed, but the guy scared Karen. He was kind of creepy. He never smiled. All he did was kind of stare, leer, and wink at her, all at once.

Karen got out of bed and put on her glasses. Great. It was only 2:45 a.m. She walked to the bedroom window, and looking out directly across the street, she noticed that the Hansens' garage door was open. Inside, two cars were parked, one of them with their headlights on and passenger door open. She saw who she thought was Mr. Hansen, but his back was to her. As he went into the house through the door in the garage, he continued to yell and struggle with something or someone. Karen got the impression that it was Mrs. Hansen. It looked like he was partly carrying and partly pushing her into the house. She must be drunk, Karen thought.

She continued to watch out of her window, wondering why the house and garage doors were still open. After about ten minutes, she saw Mr. Hansen come out of the front door of the house. He left the door open, and a moment later, a young woman came out and stood in the front yard.

Then Mr. Hansen shouted what sounded like, "She's dead."

Within two to three minutes, Karen heard the sound of sirens, which eventually stopped in front of the house. Soon she learned that what she thought she had heard was true. Janyce Hansen was dead.

* * *

Fall, 1961. Janyce was a twenty-three-year old, petite, strikingly beautiful woman. The natural brunette/sometimes blonde worked as a free-lance model and was one of Denver's best, appearing in newspaper and magazine ads and television commercials.

She was married to Eric Soltz*, and the couple had just celebrated their fourth wedding anniversary. To Janyce, however, the four years of so-called wedded bliss were four too many. When she met Eric, she had fallen fast and hard. He was good looking, in a bad-boy sort of way, and she just couldn't resist. They had a passionate relationship focused on sex. She soon realized that they had nothing else in common. She should have listened to her parents when they insisted that their Janny could do better. They always told her that she had married beneath her.

Oh well, she got two baby girls out of the deal, and they were her little treasures. Jaqueline* had just turned three, and Jill would be one in November. Janyce doted on her girls and loved being a stay-at-home mom. She hardly ever arranged for a babysitter to take care of them. If she went somewhere, the girls usually went along. She loved "prettying" them up, dressing them in matching outfits, and fixing their hair in curls and ribbons. When the three of them left the house together, she felt as if they were off to an audition. Everyone said they looked like movie stars. But as much as Janyce loved motherhood, she missed working. Now that Jill was almost one year old, she felt they could be away from their mom once in awhile. She looked forward to modeling again.

An ad in the Rocky Mountain News caught her attention. A local builder was looking for a hostess to greet clients in his model townhomes. It wasn't modeling, but it was close enough. It would get her out of the house and into socializing with adults again. She called about the job and arranged to apply the following day.

The next morning, while bathing and washing her hair, she thought about what she should wear for her interview. There was a chance they might recognize her name, and she didn't want to be hired for that alone. She dressed in a pale yellow a-line skirt that came just above her knees and a white cotton long-sleeve shirt. After she buttoned the shirt to her neck, she put on a gold multi-chain necklace. Then she gathered her hair into a ponytail at the back of her neck and tied it with a pale yellow ribbon, slipped on white flats, and took a final look in the mirror. She left the house confident that she would get the job.

"Good morning Mr. Hansen," Tina* said.

"Hey, Tina. Say, I know the ad just ran yesterday, but have we had any responses?"

"Yes, as a matter of fact we have," she replied. "Just before I left work yesterday, a woman called. I told her to stop by this morning and fill out an application. Her name's Janyce Soltz, and she said she's had experience."

"Could it be *the* Janyce Soltz, the model?" Richard replied.

"Oh, I know who you're referring to," Tina said. "I've seen her picture in different ads in the newspaper."

"She's a very attractive young woman. Tina, cancel the ad in the paper, and if anyone else calls about the job, tell them the position has been filled. If this is the Janyce we think it is, then she definitely is hired."

Richard, at the age of thirty-one, was at the top of his game. Not only was he a land developer, but he also owned real estate and several businesses. A little over six-feet tall, he was a lean, good-looking man. He had blue eyes and sandy blond hair, and although he dressed in designer suits and expensive ties, there was something sinister about his appearance. When he entered a room, his presence unnerved most people. Maybe it was his eyes, the way he seemed to look right through you. Or the way he spoke through clenched teeth—almost as if he were growling. Richard was keenly aware of how intimidating he was to others, and he liked it that way. It gave him a certain sense of power that no one else had.

A few minutes later, he heard the bell jingle on the door alerting him that someone entered the business. He walked over and opening his office door, saw Janyce. Quickly, he took off his wedding band and slipped it into his pocket as he walked over to greet her.

"Hello. Is it Ms. or Mrs. Soltz?" he asked.

"Mrs., and please call me Janyce."

"Well, it's a pleasure to meet you, Janyce. My name is Richard Hansen, but you can call me Richard."

Putting his hand on the small of her back, he led her into his office.

"Please sit down," he said, motioning to an armchair facing his desk as he walked around and sat down facing her. "When my secretary told me that a Janyce Soltz inquired about the position, I was hoping it was you. Your reputation precedes you. If it's at all possible, you are even more beautiful than your pictures."

"Thank you." She smiled and thought how typical his flattery was. Still, she sized him up. She wasn't quite sure why, but the first thing she noted was that he wasn't wearing a wedding ring. Janyce liked what she saw, and it surprised her that she could be so easily drawn to another man. She found him intriguing.

Perhaps she mistook his sinister look as confidence. In her eyes he exuded power and ambition. She didn't see a thing she didn't like about Richard Hansen.

"Well, Janyce. With you greeting our potential home buyers, they'll be asking where to sign in no time."

"Oh, does that mean I have the job?" she asked.

"Of course, I would be honored if you would accept the position."

The details were worked out, and she agreed to be there the following Monday morning at 9:00 a.m. Richard spent over an hour "interviewing" Janyce. He wanted to know as much about her as possible. She would ultimately be his. He already knew that. The fact that she was married didn't faze him in the least.

* * *

Almost immediately, the initial attraction Janyce felt for Richard began turning into much more. He was thoughtful and considerate. He brought her fresh flowers every day for her desk. He was always asking her if she wanted something to drink, or if he could get her anything.

A few weeks after she started work, he approached her, ready to make his move. He hadn't planned on seducing Janyce; after all, he was happily married and had four children. But life at home was actually pretty dull and becoming more boring as the years went by. His wife was a devout Catholic, and she was very inhibited, especially when it came to sex.

"Guess what, Janyce?" he said. "I just sold another townhome, and you deserve part of the credit, so I'm taking you out to celebrate. I thought we could have lunch and then go for a drive in the mountains."

"That sounds wonderful," she said. "My husband has been promising to take me for a drive in the hills, but so far, he hasn't found the time."

Before leaving, Richard put the convertible top down on his sports car.

"I hope you like seafood," he said as they sped away. "I know a great little place just off Colfax."

"I love seafood," she replied. "Shrimp is my favorite."

"Mine too."

They arrived within a few minutes, and the waiter, calling Richard by name, escorted them to a small table in a little nook at the far corner of the restaurant. Soon he brought over a bottle of Dom Perignon and poured them each a glass. Janyce was impressed. Dom Perignon, she thought. He must have had this planned all along.

As they drank the champagne, Richard told her about his plans to develop more land that he could build townhouses on, and how he wanted to convert apartment buildings into condos. Someday he wanted to own and operate his own restaurant.

"It sounds like you work way too hard," she told him. "Don't you ever take a break?"

"Once in a while I do like to get away on the weekends. I haven't for a long time, though. One of my favorite vacation spots is Mexico. But there's only one problem. I don't like sitting on the beach all by myself sipping Mai Tais." Reaching over, he enclosed both of her hands in his. "I know you are married, but I get a sense that you're not really happy. Would you consider going to Mexico with me some weekend?" He didn't wait for a response. Cupping Janyce's face with both his hands, he leaned over the table and kissed her on the mouth. "I'm falling in love with you, Janyce," he whispered. "Someday I'm going to take you around the world."

Janyce believed in her marriage vows, but try as she might, she could not resist Richard. Fall turned to winter, and winter to spring, and with each changing season, the love they felt for each other grew. They would often sneak into one of the bedrooms of the townhouses where Janyce was working. On occasion, Richard would reserve a hotel room, and they would spend the day together making love.

* * *

In February of 1962, Janyce made an appointment with her doctor. She had all the symptoms, and the doctor confirmed it. She was pregnant. She thought the baby was Richard's, yet there was a strong possibility that it might be Eric's. He was often away on business trips, and when he was home, although she tried to avoid having sex with him, she had to concede occasionally. Lately he had been questioning her more and more about work and about Richard.

The next morning when she arrived at work, Richard could tell something was wrong. Putting his arm around her shoulders, he led her into his office and over to the davenport.

"What is it?" he said.

"I went to the doctor yesterday and found out that I'm pregnant," Janyce said.

"The baby's mine, right? It is, isn't it?" Richard clenched his hand into a fist.

"I don't know, Richard. I want it to be yours, but I can't ignore the possibility that it's Eric's. I hated going to bed with him, but I had to submit once in a while. He's been very suspicious lately, asking me all kinds of questions. What am I going to do? What if the baby is his? What if it's yours?"

"Don't worry," he said. "I'm working on a plan for us to get married. It's just going to take a few months. In the meantime, act as normal as you can. We don't want to arouse Eric's suspicions more than we already have."

Richard went home that evening with a lot on his mind. How could he give Janyce any advice when he was in a worse predicament than she was? He kicked himself for letting things get so out of hand. How could he be so stupid? He should have told her months ago about his wife and four kids. How could he make her understand now, especially given the fact that his wife just found out that she was pregnant? He would soon be the father of five, maybe even six. He knew one thing for sure; he couldn't lose Janyce no matter what. First, he would devise a plan to get Eric out of the picture, leaving Janyce alone and vulnerable. Then she would have no choice but to forgive him. Eventually, he would have to leave his wife. And that would take some planning.

Eric made Janyce quit working for Richard when she was six months along. There was something about the man that rubbed Eric the wrong way from the first day he met him. He never liked him, and he certainly never trusted him. He only allowed Janyce to work there to keep her happy. But it was starting to get out of hand, so now was the time to put his foot down.

Eric thought he had won, but Janyce lived for the days when Eric had to go out of town on business. That was the only time she could get away to be with Richard.

It wasn't easy for Richard to stay away from her for any length of time either, but he had obligations to his family. It took some of the pressure off of him when Eric put the reins on Janyce. He could at least spend more time at home.

His wife gave birth to a baby girl on September 6, 1962. They named her Patricia*, and Richard had to play the part of a proud parent. In all respects, he loved his children, worked hard, and made sure his family wasn't in need of anything. But he also loved Janyce, and he knew he couldn't continue as he had.

He got a call from her on September 27, 1962 while he was at work.

"Hi, honey, it's me. I had the baby yesterday. A little boy. I think he looks like you. We named him John Scott Soltz, the middle name after Eric's uncle. I miss you so much, Richard. I can't wait until we're together forever."

"Soon, honey," he replied. "A few more months and we'll never have to be apart."

In the months following her son's birth, Janyce went to the townhome often. Eric never questioned her whereabouts, because she always took the kids with her. He thought she was visiting her mom or sister. Richard helped her set up a play area for her kids. They had books, toys, and games to keep them occupied while he and Janyce entertained themselves, usually in the bedroom.

For the past few weeks, he had been devising a plan to get Eric out of Janyce's life. He was ready to put his plan in motion. Before leaving the office, he placed a call to a friend.

"Hi, Gilbert*. This is Richard. Just checking to make sure you're not going to back out on me. I want to make sure everything goes exactly like we planned. Remember when you call Eric, ask for Janyce. He'll say she's not there. Then tell him you had an appointment to look at a townhome, but no one's around. Janyce was going to show it to you, and you were supposed to call that number if she wasn't there. Tell him that her car is there, so you thought you better call. Chances are he'll be so mad that Janyce is at the townhome that he won't bother to question you."

Richard had already told Janyce to get a babysitter and meet him at the townhome at noon sharp. "Plan on spending the afternoon," he told her. "I have something special planned for us."

Janyce could hardly wait. It seemed like months since she spent time alone with him. When she did, the kids were with her. She left the house knowing that she had to be back by five that evening to get dinner ready before Eric was home.

When she arrived at the townhome, Richard called for her to come into the bedroom. As she entered the room, she noticed that the blinds were drawn, and several candles were lit, creating a romantic ambiance. A bottle of champagne and three glasses sat on a table along with a few pills scattered about. The record player, turned down low, was playing romantic music. Richard walked over to her, and pulling her close, kissed her passionately.

"Whoa, sexy," Janyce said, as she gently pulled away. "What do you have on? Or what *don't* you have on?" She giggled as she pulled open one side of his white terrycloth bathrobe.

"I wore it just for you," he said. "Now, I bought you something to wear just for me. It's in the bathroom. Hurry and change. I'll be waiting."

She went into the bathroom and soon emerged wearing a skimpy transparent white baby doll top trimmed with white fake fur at the waistline. She wore matching bikini panties with garters attached to hold up white fishnet stockings. Janny blushed as she walked across the room wearing 5 inch black spike heels. She thought how *new* this life was to her. All through high school and during her marriage to Eric she was considered a prude. In comparison, Richard seemed to be open to anything--a man of the world of sorts.

Richard had to catch his breath. "Oh my God, Janyce. You are so beautiful. Sometimes I have a hard time believing you are mine."

It was everything he could do to stop himself from taking her right then and there. But he held back, wanting his plan to work out perfectly.

"Sit down, honey. Let's have a glass of champagne." He led her to one of the chairs, and he sat across from her in the other. After pouring them each a glass of champagne, he handed Janyce half of a pill.

"If this is LSD, I'm not taking it," she said.

"It's not. Come on."

He kissed her again.

"So who's the other glass for?"

"It's a surprise."

Richard poured them more champagne while he waited for the pill to take effect. He was hoping that Janyce might think she was hallucinating before she realized what was really happening. He'd have her so turned on before Gilbert arrived that she would be begging for both of them to satisfy her.

Richard picked her up and carried her over to the bed. It didn't take long until they were both sexually aroused. A short while later, Gilbert walked into the bedroom and shut the door. He took off his clothes and got into bed with them. Soon the three of them were having sex.

Suddenly, there was a loud thud. The door had swung open with such force that it hit the wall. Then the sound of Eric's voice thundered through the room. "Janyce, what in the f*** are you doing?"

As abruptly as he came into the room, he left. Janyce jumped out of bed and stumbled into the bathroom.

Gilbert got dressed. As he was leaving, Richard said, "Thanks, it worked perfectly."

Richard followed Janyce home and sat outside in his car. He wanted to make sure that Eric wouldn't cause her any trouble. A few minutes later he saw Eric come out carrying a duffle bag, get into his car, and drive away. Richard wanted to pat himself on the back. His plan had worked, and now he could have Janyce all to himself.

As Janyce and Eric divorced, Richard wanted to make sure he had control, so he started staying at her house off and on until she moved. He didn't like the idea that Eric was coming around to see the kids and wanted to make sure he didn't get any ideas of reconciling with Janyce. Richard owned several rental properties, and he was in the process of evicting one of the tenants, so he could move Janyce and her kids into the house. All the while he was slowly making the transition to get away from his wife.

Janyce's family doesn't know how long she lived with Richard before she found out that he was married and had five children—or by the same token, how long it was before Richard's wife found out that he was keeping a mistress. It may have been months, or even years, before either woman found out about the other. Maybe both women knew and were just biding their time while both of them hoped she would be the one that Richard would choose to stay with forever.

The fact is that Richard spent time with both of them at both homes while providing for both families.

TWO

In the fall of 1964, Richard moved Janyce and the kids into a small, two-bedroom house located off Hampden and Fairfax. Janyce wanted Johnny to sleep in his crib in their room and the two girls to share the other bedroom, but Richard wouldn't allow it. He didn't want Johnny, who was almost two, in their room. So he got one of the bedrooms, and the attached garage was made into a makeshift bedroom for the girls.

They laid a piece of carpet on the cold cement floor and placed two twin beds and a dresser on it. A single light bulb dangled from the ceiling with a string attached to pull it off and on. Other than that, the only source of light came from a cracked window in the old wooden door that led out to the backyard. A dutch door leading into the house from the garage was always closed, except on the rare occasions the top was left open.

Even on the nights when Richard was away, Janyce wouldn't let the girls sleep in the house for fear he would come home, find they were not in their beds, and punish them. She did leave the top half of the door open on those nights he was gone. At least then the girls felt a little more secure.

* * *

Jill hated her room in the garage, the nighttime ritual seldom varied. Their mom would tuck her and Jaqueline into bed in the freezing-cold garage with hugs and kisses. Then she would tell them, "Goodnight. Sleep tight. Don't let the bed bugs bite."

But the bed bugs did bite. Spiders, grasshoppers, crickets, and miller moths. There were tons of them. Their mom would turn the light off and go into the house, locking the door behind her.

Jill would center herself in the middle of the bed and pull the covers up to her chin. Daddy Dicky always told her that there were monsters under the bed, and if she moved, the hands would get her. "Better stay in bed," he told her, "'til I come to wake you up in the morning."

Once, in the middle of the night, Jill woke up and had to go pee. After what seemed like hours, she couldn't hold it any longer. So she got up and went to pee in the corner of the garage. She was so afraid Daddy Dicky would find out. That would be worse than any monster that might get her. After that, Jill made sure she went to the bathroom before she went to bed.

In those freezing pitch-black nights in the garage, Jill was always terrified that something or someone would come into the garage door from the backyard and get her. She would often cry herself to sleep wishing her real daddy would come and rescue her.

Although the sisters weren't allowed to sleep together, once in awhile, Jill would crawl into bed with Jaqueline. On those rare occasions, the girls always made sure Jill got back into her own bed before morning. When it was time to get up, Daddy Dicky would be the one to open the door and tell them they could come into the house. The one time he caught Jill in bed with her sister, he punished her with slaps, hits, kicks and punches, so many that she could barely move.

* * *

Life wasn't getting any better for Jill. One day, when she was about four years old, she was in the kitchen with her mother.

"Go into the bedroom and tell your Daddy Dicky that you love him," her mother said.

Jill started crying and begging, "No, don't make me go in there. Please, Mommy. I don't want to."

"Listen to me, Jill," her mother said. "Get in there, right now. You'll be just fine."

Finally, Jill did what she was told and obediently walked into the bedroom. She looked up at Richard, with tears flowing down her face.

"I love you, Daddy Dicky," she said.

"I love you too, honey. Now, close the door and come over here and sit on the bed with me."

Jill closed the door, and reluctantly walked over and stood in front of Richard. He lifted her up and sat her down beside him on the bed. Placing his hand on her thigh, he said, "You look so pretty in your cute, little, yellow dress. I bet your panties are just as pretty. He inched his hand upwards. "Can you show Daddy Dicky how pretty they are?"

"No," Jill cried out. "They're ugly. I want my mommy." She slid down from the bed and darted for the door.

Richard reached out, grabbed her by the arm, and pulled her back with such force that she fell backwards to the ground. In pain, she began crying for her mom.

Janyce heard her daughter's cries and was torn. She wanted to go to Jill, but yet she wanted to avoid any confrontation with Richard, so she went outside.

Richard got up off the bed and kicked Jill, as he walked around her toward the door. "Quit your damn crying, or I'll give you something else to cry about." As he left the room, he yelled out for Janyce, "Jill's crying like she's getting killed, and all she did was trip and fall."

In the hours that followed the ordeal, Jill complained to her mother that her arm hurt. Janyce thought it would eventually be okay. When Jill was still complaining of the pain two days later, Janyce decided to take her to the doctor and discovered that her daughter's arm was indeed broken. She was sent home with a cast on her arm. It's difficult to image what Janyce felt, or if she were too terrified of Richard to let herself feel anything.

When Richard saw the cast, he warned Jill, "You damn well better not tell anyone what really happened, or else. If anyone does ask you, tell them that you fell down and broke it. If you don't, I'll take you into the bedroom again."

* * *

Sometimes Janyce wished her life could go back to the way it was before she met Richard, before he had so much control over her. She wasn't allowed to do anything without his consent, not groceries, not shopping for clothes. He was always lurking nearby. In the past, she enjoyed the friendship she had with Helen*, her only sister. But Richard didn't like Janyce being close to anyone but him, so he always tried to come up with some excuse to keep her away from anyone in her family.

At other times, Janyce loved Richard more than anything in the world. He could be so good to her, treating her like a princess, showering her with little gifts and flowers. She especially liked it when he would surprise her by telling her they were going away for the weekend.

Whether it was a jaunt to the mountains, a drive to California, or flying to Mexico, Janyce loved that Richard included her children on their getaways. Sometimes, though, his sense of family values was a little twisted. Richard often took them out to dinner and then to the movies. Yet he would make the kids wait outside in the back of the theater by the exit door while he paid for Janyce and him to get in. When the movie started, he would sneak the kids in through the exit door.

He also took the family many times to see the Denver Rockets play basketball. Even though he had plenty of cash, Jill, Jaqueline, and Johnny had to sneak in. He told them, "If you want to get in, you have to walk by the guy who is taking the tickets. If he doesn't let you in, you have to go back to the car while we watch the game."

Although the kids were scared, they walked right in. Maybe Richard did pay for them and just wanted them to think they were doing something wrong. He did enjoy playing these little games with them, and he got a kick out of watching their fear.

One night, the five of them went in to watch the game.

After they sat down, Johnny said to his dad, "I have to go to the bathroom."

"Hold it Johnny, because we are not going," Richard said.

The two of them went back and forth, with Richard elbowing Johnny in his side and telling him to shut up.

The guy sitting behind them said, "Take your kid to the bathroom already."

Richard turned to face the man. "You have no right telling me what to do with my kid." Right after that, he told Janyce to leave with the kids and he would find his own way home.

Richard waited until the game was over, and then followed the guy outside. He tapped him on the shoulder and hollered, "Nobody tells me what to do, you son of a bitch."

Before the man had a chance to defend his actions, Richard pummeled him with both fists and laid him out cold. As the man lay unconscious, Richard began kicking him. By this time, a crowd had gathered, and a few men stepped up to pull him back.

"Stop, mister," one of them yelled. "He's not moving. You're going to kill him."

About that time the police arrived and arrested Richard. As they hauled him off to jail, he fought and threatened. Later, an officer brought him home. The charges didn't stick, and it appeared that Richard used his power of persuasion—or one of his numerous connections—to escape punishment.

* * *

One of the first family getaways in 1967 was to Laguna Beach, California. Richard rented a small townhouse on a hilltop. Janyce's three children were about five, seven and nine years old. Janyce was going out to do some shopping and took Jill and Johnny with her. Jaqueline had to stay behind with Richard, and she begged Jill to stay there with her. Jill, however, had to go with her mom and brother.

No matter how much Jaqueline begged to go with them, her mom said, "I'm sorry, but you can't go. Richard wants you to stay here and keep him company."

Thinking back to that day, Jill realizes that Richard must have already been sexually abusing Jaqueline, and that Janyce must have been aware of it.

While at the townhouse, the next day Richard took Janyce and her three kids to a restaurant for dinner. They had to walk down a steep hill from their townhouse to get there. Richard took hold of Johnny's and Jill's hands, and they started walking. He went faster and faster until they were running. It was fun at first, but their little legs couldn't keep up, and they begged him to stop. Richard kept running and ended up partially dragging them down the hill. By the time they had reached the bottom, both kids had bloody knees and were crying.

Snickering, Richard said, "Shut up and be quiet, or I'll give you something to cry about."

THREE

Apparently, Janyce discovered that Richard was married in the fall of 1968. Her parents somehow found out about it and tried to convince her to leave him. They were starting to see a different side to Richard, a side they didn't like. So, whether or not he manipulated the situation by arranging for them to find out, or whether they did some digging and found out on their own, their discovery worked to his advantage, because it put him in a position to call the shots.

As soon as he found out that Janyce's parents were trying to split them up, he demanded she break all contact with them. She was not even allowed to speak with them on the phone. This was only temporary, a few months at most, but it gave Richard much more power over his second family. Until then, no one who mattered was aware that he had a wife and five children at home.

Was it strategic planning or merely a peace offering to console Janyce after she found out about his marriage? Either way, it worked. Janyce was thrilled to find out he had arranged for the two of them to take a four-week vacation around the world. Of course, she would forgive him. Richard chose to take her on that trip, and not his wife.

While they were off having the time of their lives, her children were not as fortunate. They were left home alone to fend for themselves. By this time, they had moved into a larger house Richard had built for them on Locust Street in Denver. The girls' bedroom was in the house, not in the garage.

Jaqueline, age ten, was left in charge of her two siblings, Jill age eight, and John age six. Her duties included getting them up and ready for school, giving them breakfast, and making sure they all went to school every day and arrived home on time. After school, it was homework, cooking dinner and making sure they were all bathed and in bed by 8:30 p.m. This was a lot for anyone to handle, let alone a child.

Richard's mother stopped by the house occasionally to check on the kids, do a little cleaning, and make sure they had enough food. But she was like a stranger to them. Although she was nice enough, they had seen her only a few times and knew her only as Richard's mother. They wished their Grandma and Grandpa Bloom would come and get them, but they knew that Daddy Dicky had made sure that wouldn't happen.

It's unknown if Janyce knew the kids would be left alone, or if she willingly went along with it. It is difficult to comprehend that a mother could knowingly leave her children alone to fend for themselves for even a day—certainly not for four weeks.   To the children, it seemed like months before their mom came home. As far as Richard and Janyce were concerned, the four weeks went by quickly. They returned to find everything in order. Although the children looked well physically, their ordeal served to redefine the insecurity that Jill had to cope with every day of her life.

* * *

Janyce fell back into the routine of being a mother. It was important to her and Richard that the kids get a good education, and she was determined that they go to school every day. She made sure they were always clean and well dressed before they left the house.

Jill had been diagnosed with a nervous stomach, and she would throw up at least once a week, often in the classroom. She also suffered from nightmares almost every night. One particular evening, she was more afraid than usual and needed to be comforted by her mom. She stayed awake in bed for the longest time, waiting for her fear to subside so she could go to her mom's bedroom. She knew that the door would be locked, because Daddy Dicky said that kids were never allowed inside. But she hoped that her mom would get up for her this time.

Finally, she got up the nerve and crept to their bedroom. She knocked softly on the door, hoping her mom would hear.

"Who's out there?" Daddy Dicky yelled.

"I need my mommy," Jill cried.

"Your mommy is sleeping. Get back to bed—now—or I'll give you something to cry about."

Too afraid to go back to her room, Jill curled herself into a ball on the floor next to the door and eventually fell asleep.

The next morning, she woke up feeling pain in her ribs. Daddy Dicky, already dressed, with his boots on, was kicking her. She jumped up and ran to her room with Daddy Dicky right behind her kicking her all the way. He didn't stop until he had Jill cornered in her room.

"There, you little brat," he shouted. "Now you have something to cry about."

She continued to sob, and soon he returned, picked her up, and half-dragging her, threw her onto the bed. Getting down on his knees, he glared at Jill with all the hate he could muster. "I better not ever catch you sleeping in front of my bedroom door again, or else."

Jill was terrified. Life couldn't get any worse, she thought.

FOUR

In January of 1971, Richard and Janyce were married. He was thirty-nine, and Janyce was thirty-three. The children, John, Jill and Jaqueline, were eight, ten and twelve years old. They still had no idea Richard had been married once before, nor did they know about his five children.

Because she was divorced, Janyce didn't want an elaborate event, and they decided to get married at the City Hall. Janyce's sister, Helen, and her husband, Ted*, stood up with them. They celebrated with drinks and dinner after the wedding vows.

By this time, the family had settled into their larger house. Each of the three children had a bedroom.

Although Janyce seemed happy, something was nagging at Richard. He didn't like that she still took her kids to see their dad. Now that they were married, he wanted to make sure that he could keep his hold on her. What better way to do that than through her children?

After Janyce divorced her first husband, Richard had allowed her to take the children to see him but with restrictions. The only place they could visit him was at a local country club in Denver where he worked as a chef. Janyce would take them there, and he made time away from the kitchen to visit them briefly at their table.

Used to having complete control over everything and everyone around him, Richard didn't like the fact that Janyce was seeing her ex, no matter what the circumstances. To get his way, he made arrangements to adopt Jaqueline, Jill and John. No one knows why Eric would so readily give up his kids, and it is rumored that Richard used threats, money or both.

He held power over anyone he came in contact with, and he had considerable resources at his disposal. By whatever means, he had accomplished what he set out to do. Eric was forced into relinquishing all rights to his children, and the adoption was finalized late February 1971. Richard took the necessary steps to make sure that Johnny, the youngest child, would not be connected to Eric in any way. The new birth certificate would omit the middle name of Scott, and Johnny would be John Hansen.

* * *

In April of 1971, Richard took Janyce and his new family down to Juarez, Mexico. At that time, Mexico wasn't much of a tourist attraction, especially not Juarez. The kids thought it was dirty and gross. They sure didn't want to eat the food or drink the water. Only their hotel, the Camino Real, felt safe.

When they went for dinner that evening at a French restaurant, they noticed only a handful of other Americans. The owner came over to the table and introduced himself.

"Would you like a salad with your meal?" he asked.

"No, thank you," Richard replied. "We're not sure about eating all the food here."

"Would you follow me, please?" His gaze traveled around the table at all five of them. "I'd like to show you our kitchen so that you'll understand how we prepare our food."

And that's exactly what he did. Giving them a crash course on food preparation, the owner guided them around the facility. They saw how clean everything was and observed the water filtration system and how the vegetables were washed.

From then on, they all loved Mexico and vowed to return many times as a family.

* * *

It was the summer of 1971. Jill was ten years old. She lay in bed having a hard time falling asleep. She couldn't get used to sleeping alone. In their old house, she shared a room with Jaqueline. Thinking about that now was scary. She remembered waking up one night and seeing Daddy Dicky in Jaqueline's bed. She lay there silently and tried to block out the sounds of him grunting and moaning. After he left the room, her sister sobbed into her pillow.

"What happened?" Jill had asked her.

"Leave me alone," Jaqueline said, no longer crying, just really angry. "And you shut up. Don't say anything to anyone, or you'll be sorry."

Daddy Dicky returned to Jaqueline's bed on numerous occasions. Each time, Jill would pretend she didn't hear. And each time he left, Jaqueline would cry.

Not long after, Jill had just about fallen asleep when she heard the creak of her bedroom door slowly opening. It was a warm summer night. Her bedroom window was open, and the moonlight coming through it cast an eerie glow on Daddy Dicky, as he slowly approached her bed. She wanted to scream out in terror. Instead, she closed her eyes and screamed in her head, *"Please help me, Mommy."*

She laid there, her body motionless, silently praying that he would go away. He walked to the side of her bed and knelt down on his knees. Jill sensed his presence and could feel his breath on the side of her face. She kept her eyes squeezed tightly shut. *Leave,* she thought. *Just leave.*

Richard savored every moment of her fear, as he slowly reached his fingers out to stroke her long brown hair. He leaned his face over and gently brushed his lips along her cheek. Putting his mouth against her ear, he whispered, "Daddy Dicky wants to make you happy, Jill. Just keep your eyes closed and don't say anything." He reached down to lift her nightgown. While doing so, he touched her leg, and she jolted and began to cry.

He chuckled. "It's okay, honey," he said. "I'm going to show you how much I love you."

Then he lifted her nightgown to her waist, reached his fingers into her panties, and touched her.

Suddenly, Jill cried out. She couldn't help it. She was terrified.

"Shut up and quit crying," he demanded with his usual threat. "Or I'll give you something to cry about."

Jill only sobbed louder.

"Okay, you little brat," he told her. "I'll leave you alone tonight, but the next time I come back, you better not cry, or I'll hurt you real bad, and then I'll kill your little brother."

After that, he returned to her bedroom at least once a week, becoming more aggressive with each visit. Ultimately, he forced her to do everything and anything that he wanted.

"Just do what I tell you to," he said, "or you know what will happen to you and your brother."
Over the next five years, Jill was forced to suffer through the pain and humiliation of his every desire.

* * *

In August of 1971, the family was off to Mexico again. This time Richard took them to Puerto Vallarta. He enjoyed showing his new family a good time by taking them to many different places and spending a lot of money, but he also wouldn't allow for anyone to stay happy for very long. It seemed to John and Jill that he got his kicks from watching the fear he could evoke in them.

He especially liked the fact that there were no rules regarding underage drinking in Mexico. He would take his family out to eat and order them all margaritas. At first, the kids thought it was fun to drink with their parents, but soon the grown-up feeling lost its appeal.

"Come on," Richard would insist. "Have another one."

If they slowed down, he'd kick them under the table. If Janyce noticed, she didn't indicate it. She was drinking as well.

When they left the restaurant, the kids would be throwing up as they staggered along. If they fell down, he would laugh and kick at them until they got up. This would continue until they finally arrived at the hotel. Once they were ready for bed, the antics continued. The kids were forced to entertain Daddy Dicky until either they collapsed or until he passed out.

FIVE

Still, some of Richard's actions bothered her. She didn't like how mean he was to the kids. Although he had always disciplined them, it seemed that now he just wanted to hurt them. He was also becoming more abusive toward her and would find any excuse and hit her or elbow her, usually in the stomach. She always had bruises, which she concealed under her clothes.

What bothered her most was that many nights she would wake up and realize he wasn't in bed with her. Lying awake, she would listen for him. One night she thought she heard noises coming from one of the girls' bedrooms, but she was too frightened to go and look. Although she had her suspicions as to what Richard might be doing, she would push those thoughts to the back of her mind. Had Richard always been like that? Maybe she hadn't noticed because she was so in love with him. True, he made it easy for her to love him. But then again, he made it easy for her not to.

Richard wouldn't allow her to go anywhere without him, so unless she went with him, she was stuck in the house all day. He had allowed her to take a few modeling jobs in the past. Of course, he would drop her off at the job and pick her up when she was finished. She did it mostly for the satisfaction it gave her, and one job did prove to be lucrative. She had done a few photo shoots and modeling jobs with Johnny when he was a baby, and the photographs were used for advertising. One appeared on a pacifier package in stores for many years. Janyce loved that kind of work, but she knew Richard would never allow her to do it now.

Richard was making a great deal of money in the seventies, thanks to Denver's energy boom. Skyscrapers, shopping malls, and suburban subdivisions were being built everywhere.

Richard Hansen Enterprises jumped on the gravy train and soon became a successful real estate development firm. One of the projects Richard was credited for building was the Applewood Village Townhouses in Lakewood, Colorado. Then he hired architect Roland Wilson to work on several other projects with him and continued to build apartment complexes and subdivisions, including developing the subdivision where he built their next family home.

Soon he started planning the construction of The Cannery Restaurant in Denver. He purchased a parcel of land off I25 and Yale. In January 1972, he and Janyce loaded up the three kids, and they set off for a drive in the Rocky Mountains. It was one of several weekend trips they made over the course of the month in search of materials for the construction of the restaurant. Richard and Janyce envisioned The Cannery with a rustic exterior of old barn wood, or something with a similar appearance, and they hoped it would become a five-star restaurant serving the finest steak and lobster.

Since they weren't having any luck in the mountains finding the type of wood they wanted, Richard and Janyce made a trip to California's Carmel and Monterey area. There they found an old building that was perfect for their needs. They purchased it and arranged to have the wood shipped back to Denver.

They oversaw all aspects of building The Cannery and planned to put all their efforts into making the restaurant a success. Richard and Janyce wanted to be there often showing the employees moral support and making sure the customers were enjoying the food and having a good time. Richard told the children that when The Cannery was completed, they would hold a grand opening, and that he had a special surprise in store for them.

Jill hated whenever Daddy Dicky said he had a surprise. It started as something fun, but Jill knew bad things would happen later. To her, it meant he would come into her room when she was sleeping, just as he had been doing for the past year.

By August of 1972, the restaurant was perfect, and it was time for the grand opening. On that evening, Richard told John, Jill, and

Jaqueline to get cleaned up and to dress in their best, because he was going to give them the surprise that he had promised them. He was planning to introduce them to his other five children.

Janyce took the three kids to The Cannery to wait for Richard. A dinner table was set for ten. John, Jill, and Jaqueline had not been told anything about their sisters and brothers, only that there were five of them.

Janyce had previously met with his children on several occasions. They weren't all ready to accept her as their stepmother. Indeed, she thought, they hated her, especially the three oldest ones. They couldn't accept her because they believed that she had stolen their father away from them and their mother. The two youngest ones didn't seem to mind as much.

Richard showed up for dinner with only two of the kids, explaining that the other three were not interested.

"When I went to pick them up, Niles* and Kathy* refused to come along," he said. "Linda* was going to, but she decided to jump out of the car at a stoplight, so I just brought Patricia and David*".

The four younger kids got along great. Jill and David were both eleven years old, and John and Patricia were both nine. Being they were all so close in ages, they found that they shared some of the same interests. Jill and David seemed to overlook the fact that they were brother and sister through adoption, and started to think of themselves as potential girlfriend and boyfriend. Jill only hoped that David had no idea what Richard had done to her those horrible nights in her room.

Janyce enjoyed the children and looked forward to including them in their family. Much of the evening was spent discussing future trips they would take.

"Fun," Janyce told Jill and anyone else who was listening. "We're all going to have so much fun together."

SIX

In late August of 1972, Richard was looking forward to the annual fishing trip to Saratoga, Wyoming. It had become a family tradition for Adolph, Niles, David, and him to make the trip every year in August, and now he could finally take Johnny along. They would have the van packed and ready to go and be on the road at dawn for the four-hour long drive. The guys would stay for about a week at the Saratoga Inn Motel. Every morning they would get up at the crack of dawn and drive the short distance to the North Platte River, where they would set up camp for the day and fish for trout.

The first morning they arrived, they unloaded the van, put on their waders, strapped their creels around their shoulders, and headed down toward the river. To Johnny, it felt peaceful and tranquil, as if they must be the only ones around for miles. Then they split up. Richard, Adolph, and Niles stayed together, and Johnny and David went upstream.

Richard, Adolph, and Niles were just getting ready to cast off when the sound of gunfire shattered the peaceful quiet. They hit the ground as they watched a man come running over the bridge firing a shotgun in the direction of Johnny and David. The man was about sixty, and his shoulder-length gray hair was scraggly and dirty. He wore an unbuttoned red-and-black flannel shirt and overalls, which were held up with suspenders. Apparently, he'd lacked the time to tie his rubber boots, as they seemed ready to fall off as he ran down the hill toward them.

"What was that?" Johnny yelled at David.

"Johnny," David shouted. "We're getting shot at. Let's get the hell out of here. Come on, let's go."

They reeled up their rods as fast as they could and took off running downstream through the woods. The trees were rustling off to the side of them. Suddenly, through the clearing, a deer jumped out in front of them, and they all thought for a moment, that it was the guy with the shotgun. They ran as fast as they could, yelling for Richard.

The old man was about fifty yards away when he shot at them.

"Get the hell out of here, you sons-a-bitches," he yelled as he ran. "I'll shoot you myself and bury you. No one would ever come looking for you on private property."

John and David ran as fast as their legs would carry them and dove for cover next to their dad. Lying face-down on the ground, with their hands on their heads, they screamed, "Don't shoot. Please."

Richard was scared, as he showed both hands and slowly got up to face the man.

"Please don't shoot, mister. Just listen. I have lots of money. I'm from Denver, and I know a lot of important people. I'll pay you for the use of your land, and I can give you whatever you want."

The mention of money seemed to spark the old man's interest, and he calmed down.

After some discussion, Richard paid the man, and they continued to fish on his land for years to come. Without the promise of more money each time they came back, Richard believed the man may have killed them all, right then and there, just for the sport of it.

And that was just Johnny's introduction to his father's lifestyle. Richard portrayed himself as a good husband and father. He included his wife and children in almost everything from vacations to helping out in the family business. Other people envied them, and why not? They were the rich and beautiful, fun-loving family. Who wouldn't want to be like them? No one, if they only knew the kind of man Richard really was.

He insisted that his children be knowledgeable in many areas, including horseback riding, swimming, snorkeling, scuba diving, tubing, rafting, and skiing. He was the teacher, and what a fickle teacher he was. If you got on a horse, he would hit the horse in the rear causing it to run or buck. If you were getting ready to ski down a slope, he would push you. If he wanted to teach you to swim, he would throw you in the water. His belief was that you learned how to do it, or died trying.

* * *

Soon after they returned from the fishing trip, Richard planned to take Janyce and the kids to Puerto Vallarta before school started. Johnny, Jill, Patricia, and David were the only other ones going with them. Richard drove their green van down to Mexico, taking his time and stopping at several places along the way.

When they reached Puerto Vallarta, Richard rented a house on the beach. It came with a maid and cook, so there was nothing to do but have fun. Richard and Janyce could easily communicate with the staff and the locals, and the children spoke the language well enough to get by.

The family spent a lot of time snorkeling and scuba diving. One day when the kids were all playing on the beach and in the ocean, Richard sent Janyce up to the house to have the maid make them each a drink. He was about waist-deep in the water when he called to Jill, "Come over here. I want to see how your backstroke is coming along."

Jill's stomach dropped. She felt sick as he leered at her, and she knew full well that he didn't have her backstroke in mind.

"Hurry up," he said.

Jill obediently made her way toward him, and he grew excited as he watched her paddle through the water. Her long brown hair hung in strands as it clung to her shoulders. She was wearing a red two-piece swimsuit, and her developing breasts were marked by her top, which was tied tightly at her back.

As she neared him, she turned onto her back, ready to push out past him into the deeper water. Then his hand shot up from under the surface, and he grabbed the bottom of her swimsuit pulling it partially down.

"Oh no," he said. "You're not getting away from me. You know what Daddy Dicky wants. Show Daddy your sidestroke, Jill."

She stretched out her arms and lifted off with her feet.

Richard held onto her arm with one hand, while groping her between her legs with his other. She tried pulling away from him, but he grabbed her tightly around the waist and pulled her close to him. Jill's back was to Richard, and she could feel his hardness, as he pressed his body against her. She tried pushing his hand away from her crotch, which only seemed to excite him more, as he continued rubbing against her.

"Stop," she said and looked frantically around for help.

"Shut up," he replied. "If you say another word, I'll drown Johnny. Now, let's see your sidestroke."

Again, she looked around for a way out. Finding none, she closed her eyes tightly and gritted her teeth.

Richard kept it up. "Come on, Jill—kick, kick faster."

Then Jill heard her mother yelling, "Richard, here are the drinks."

She opened her eyes to see her mom walking from the house down to the water.

"I'll be right there," Richard called back. "I was just helping Jill with her sidestroke." He turned to Jill, and through clenched teeth, quietly said, "Smile, you little bitch, and get the hell out of here."

Jill went and lay face-down on the beach, then cried herself to sleep.

* * *

That same evening Richard and Janyce went out for dinner and drinks. David and Jill also left the house to hang out with the local kids. That left Johnny and Patricia, who were only ten years old and not allowed to leave.

As kids will do, when left alone to their own devices, they cooked up a plan. They wanted to have fun too, so they decided to go get some beer. This was more Johnny's idea than Patricia's. Her dad hadn't introduced her to drinking yet, but she was game. So off they walked to the nearest grocery store, where they purchased a six pack. It was early in the evening, so they thought they had plenty of time to drink the beer before going back to the house.

It was almost midnight when they decided they'd had enough. Both drunk, they staggered along the road as they hurried to get home before their parents did. They weren't quick enough, though. As they saw headlights approaching, they realized it was the van. Richard pulled up alongside them, and the kids didn't have time to think.

"Get home now, boy," Richard shouted.

The van sped off, and the two ran home as fast as their rubbery legs would go. Richard was standing there waiting for them when they walked into the house, and the other kids were also home.

Richard had his eye on Johnny as he slowly pulled his belt off. Then he grabbed him by the arm and took him to the bedroom, where he beat his butt until it was black and blue. Richard wasn't mad at the fact that his kids were drinking. He was mad because they left the house without his permission.

Jill and Patricia heard everything, as they sat in their bedroom on the bed holding onto each other while Johnny was being beaten.

When Jill saw Johnny sulking around the next morning, she asked, "Are you okay? Patricia and I heard you screaming and crying last night."

"Dad beat me with a belt," he said, "and he didn't touch his precious Patricia. She didn't even get in trouble. He didn't yell at her or anything. I'm glad he's not my real dad. I hate him. Where is our real dad, Jill? How come we don't see him anymore? Doesn't he love us?"

Jill thought about it before answering. It had been several months since they last saw their dad, and she missed him more than anything. She wished he were here so she could tell him how unhappy she was and what Daddy Dicky made her do. There was only one reason why they didn't see him anymore. Daddy Dicky wouldn't allow it. That's what the adoption was all about, but she couldn't tell that to Johnny. They would probably never see their real dad again. But she needed to protect her little brother. She gave him a quick hug.

"We'll probably see him soon," she said.

* * *

After their vacation, Richard and Janyce went to work at The Cannery. The next few years were focused on making the restaurant a success. The weekend getaways continued, with as many of Richard's other children as chose to go. David and Patricia would usually accompany them. The other three children were still uncertain about their father's relationship with a woman other than their mother, so they usually chose to stay at home.

Richard continued to abuse Jill, and she wasn't sure how long she could stay silent. She had to, though. If she confided in anyone, he would kill Johnny. That's what he'd told her. He would kill her brother.

SEVEN

It was early 1973, and drugs and alcohol were still playing a huge role in Richard's volatile nature. To the kids, it seemed the more he drank, the meaner he was to them and their mom.

When Jill was twelve years old, Jaqueline ran away from home. Jill was devastated. She wondered who she could turn to now. Although the girls never spoke to each other about what their adopted father did to them, they were both keenly aware that the other one knew. Somehow, it gave Jill a selfish sense of comfort knowing she wasn't the only one who had to put up with the pain and humiliation of Daddy Dicky's perversion.

She especially missed her big sister when she had to walk to school alone. It made her sad to think that Jaqueline couldn't even go to classes anymore, all because of Daddy Dicky. Now, when she walked to school, David and his friends picked on her, because he didn't like the fact that Jill called his dad names. True, Jill must have called him every name in the book the night he beat Jaqueline up because Jaqueline finally told her mom the truth about what he had been doing to her for years.

When Richard started beating Jaqueline, Jill, Johnny, and David all ran into David's bedroom. All three of them sat on the bed crying and scared as they wondered what they could do. Jaqueline was crying and screaming for her mom to come and help her. Daddy Dicky kept beating her, insisting that she was just trying to cause trouble by telling all her lies.

Jill heard her mom come out of her bedroom as the fighting and screaming rose to a fearful crescendo. Her mom raced down the hall toward the living room screaming at Daddy Dicky.

"Stop," she shouted.

"I'll stop, all right."

He let Jaqueline go and started beating on their mom.

Jill ran out of the bedroom and down the hall.

"You're a sick pig," she yelled at him. "Leave my mom alone."

She watched as he loosened his grip on her mom's neck and pushed her to the ground, knocking over a table and lamp as she fell.

Jill knew there was nothing more she could do to help her mom, so she went to check on Jaqueline. Her sister looked terrible with two black eyes starting to swell. Blood ran out of her nose and both ears. Jaqueline went into Johnny's room, and Jill followed. Jaqueline hugged her and said "I'm sorry. I can't stay here any longer", and then Jill watched as her sister climbed out the window.

Jaqueline turned and said, "I love you." Then she ran down the block and out of sight.

The commotion in the house died down until a couple hours later when Richard discovered that Jaqueline wasn't home. Then all hell broke loose again.

"We better go find your lying little whore daughter," he shouted at Janyce. "We need to get her ass home before the little bitch has a chance to spread more of her lies around."

They eventually found Jaqueline and brought her home, only to have her run away again. She went to the only people she could trust, her grandparents, Ben and Molly, and her Aunt Helen and Uncle Ted*. This time Richard didn't want her back in the house. He also forbade Janyce, Jill, and Johnny from speaking with her on the phone, or from ever seeing her again. Janyce was also not to speak to or see her parents or sister.

* * *

In the early fall of 1974, Richard and Janyce had been working long hours at The Cannery and decided to take a much needed vacation, another trip around the world. On this particular trip, the kids were older and didn't mind being left at home alone, especially Jill. She looked forward to going to bed at night without worrying about Daddy

Dicky getting into bed with her. She was almost fourteen and in charge of babysitting Johnny, who was in the sixth grade at the time. Helen's daughter, Brenda*, was staying with them to help out. She was a couple of years older than Jill. Johnny didn't like the idea of having two girls babysitting him, but he decided to make the best of it.

The morning after their parents left, Johnny got up and got ready for school and came into the kitchen. Brenda was already up and in the kitchen preparing breakfast.

"Morning, Johnny. Look what I have," she said, as she set something on the kitchen table.

Looking at it curiously, Johnny observed a large glass object with a tube thing in it.

"What the heck is that thing?" he asked.

"It's what you're going to have with your breakfast," Brenda replied.

"What do you do with that?"

Johnny watched as she lit a match, and the thing started smoking. She inhaled. "Try it, Johnny. It's far out."

He copied her, and it wasn't long before his head started spinning. He sat back in his chair and closed his eyes, praying to himself that the feeling would quickly pass. After awhile, he thought he better go to school while he was still able. He gathered his things and flashed his cousin the peace sign as he went out the door.

Johnny managed to make it through the day at school, although, at first, he doubted if he could. At one point, he started perspiring so profusely that he took off his shirt in the middle of class. The teacher led him into the hall to get a drink of water. She never did find out what was wrong with him.

That day was a turning point for him. It was basically downhill from there with drugs, alcohol, and everything else in his life. Growing up with Richard as his father was terrifying for Johnny. His dad was scary, abusive, demanding, and controlling. Just the sound of his voice made Johnny cringe. If you did something he didn't like, you didn't get yelled at or grounded. You got beaten. Whatever was handy, his dad would put to use, a shoe, a belt, or anything he could grab. More often than not, he used his fists.

* * *

Just before Johnny's thirteenth birthday, he was sitting in the backyard with his dad, when out of the blue, Richard said, "You know, Johnny, you have my hair."

He looked over at his dad's balding head. "God, I hope not."

Richard busted into laughter. Trying to compose himself, he looked at Johnny with a straight face. "You are my real son," he said.

Johnny freaked out and started to cry. He ran towards the house screaming for his mother. "Mom, Richard just told me I'm his real son. I thought Eric was my real dad. What's going on?"

Johnny spent many years trying to come to terms with the fact that Richard was his biological father and to sort out his feelings about it. Although he didn't see Eric very often, he knew he was his dad, and he loved him. Now, all of a sudden, he had to accept Richard as his dad. Forever. Johnny hated it and him.

Johnny's mom wasn't as scary, but lately it seemed she was following in Richard's footsteps when it came to hurting him. Her weapon of choice was a hairbrush. If there wasn't one handy, he could count on getting kicked. At the time, Johnny thought all parents treated their kids like that.

* * *

A couple of months after Richard and Janyce had returned from their trip around the world, Richard came up with, what he thought, was a brilliant idea to utilize the extra space in the house now that Jaqueline was gone. He had a plan for a business he could operate right from the comfort of his own home. What would be especially gratifying is it involved everything that he loved: money, women, and sex. He would turn his Locust Street home into a brothel, and he would be the pimp. He couldn't believe he hadn't thought of the idea before.

It was easy enough to get the business going. He already knew a handful of girls who were eager to work for him. He also knew plenty of potential clients. The girls would work out of his home. They would be sent to a prearranged designated place, such as a hotel, or to a client's home. They could do the job and then bring back the money to him. Richard set up a phone line and called his business Playmates Unlimited. He needed assistants, so he trained Jill and Janyce on how to answer the phone when clients called. Jill blushed as Richard told her in vivid detail what the call girls were and what their duties would entail. Later he whispered in Jill's ear, "Someday you'll be good enough to do their job."

Richard's call girls were beautiful and came with a high price tag. Soon, business was booming, and he was making thousands of dollars. Janyce didn't have any say in what was going on. She had to put up with all of the whores in her house. Jill thought that the women were beautiful, and Johnny thought it was great. He would often invite his friends over just to gawk at the girls.

Richard even had his basement transformed into what he liked to refer to as his "den of inequity." The girls spent most of their time there when they weren't working. That's also where Richard spent most of his time, usually hosting an orgy.

By the spring of 1975, he decided to close the doors on Playmates Unlimited. The Cannery was starting to suffer as a result of his not being there. When he started pimping, he had basically handed over control of the restaurant's daily operations to his employees. He believed that it could run itself, and he was now paying for that mistake.

In an attempt to right that wrong, he started working at The Cannery every day, sometimes staying until four in the morning, only to go home, get up the next morning, and start again.

For the last year, Richard and Janyce both had been working day and night at The Cannery. Finally, all their hard work was starting to pay off. The restaurant was thriving again—but, the long hours and endless days were starting to take a toll on them, and they decided to get out of the restaurant business. They leased out the property, and it became Sam Wilson's Meat Market Restaurant.

EIGHT

September 26, 1975 was the big one for Johnny. He was thirteen years old. Waking with the realization that he was finally a teenager, he jumped out of bed, walked over to the mirror, and pulled up his new bell bottoms. They were a little long, but his mom bought them that way because she said he was growing like a weed. Johnny looked close into the mirror, feeling his chin for any signs of new hair growth, *peach fuzz,* as his dad called it.

Then he picked up the comb to straighten the middle part in his hair. He didn't have any trouble growing that. He liked his hair. It was sandy blond, with a light wave, and it was almost down to his shoulders. He laid the comb down, grabbed his socks and a long-sleeve shirt, and then headed for the kitchen.

He was feeling full of himself as he poured a bowl of cereal. Heck, he might even start smoking today. He sat down at the table to eat, and his mom came over and tousled his hair.

"Happy birthday," she told him.

His dad just ignored him, and his sister, Jill, was in the bathroom getting ready for school. That didn't seem right. He kind of expected everyone to make a big deal of his birthday, especially the fact that he was now a teenager.

While walking to school, he wondered why his dad had to be such a jerk. Maybe he was still mad about the stick deal. The family had spent the past weekend in Breckenridge at their ski-in, ski-out townhouse, The Christiana. Just him, Jill, and his mom and dad. It was

September, so they spent their time just hanging out and exploring. Johnny happened to find a really neat stick, almost five-feet long, and a couple of inches thick.

When they were packed and ready to go home on Sunday, he had carried the walking stick to the van. His dad saw it and said, "What the hell is that, Johnny?"

"My walking stick. Isn't it cool?" He climbed into the van.

"No, it's not cool, and I don't want it in my vehicle. Throw the damn thing out now."

"Oh, Richard," his mom had said. "It's not hurting anything. And his birthday is tomorrow. Let him keep it." His dad didn't say anything else about it, so Johnny brought it home.

By the time he got to school that day, he had worked himself into a state thinking about it, and he took his attitude into math class with him. The kids were taking a test, and a boy sitting next to Johnny asked him a question. Johnny whispered back a reply.

"Quiet," the teacher said.

The boy said something again, and the teacher heard Johnny reply back to him.

"I said, be quiet."

She was starting to get on his nerves.

He leaned over to retrieve a pencil he had dropped on the floor and mumbled under his breath, "Aw, shut up, you f***ing bitch."

The students broke into laughter.

"What?" the teacher demanded. "Excuse me, young man. I heard what you said. You need to go to the principal's office right now."

Johnny was suspended from school for the remainder of the week, and his mom picked him up. Birthday or not, he knew he was in for some kind of punishment. When they arrived home, his mom pulled up in front of the house.

"Get out and go inside," she said.

Then she drove away, and he knew that it was going to be bad.

Johnny walked into the house alone, with quiet resolve. He was ready for whatever his dad had planned for him. Over time, after each beating, it was as if he had slowly built up an emotional callous that covered his body. This time he was determined not to cry.

His parents' bedroom was in the lower part of the house. No one else was at home, and Johnny sensed that his dad was in his bedroom. He walked over to the stairway.

"Hey, Dad," he called.

"I'll be right up," his father answered.

Johnny went over and sat on the arm rest of the couch while he waited. His dad sounded way too calm, which was scarier to him than if he were yelling. Johnny's resolve to take it like a man was fading fast, as he heard his dad coming up the stairs.

Finally towering over Johnny, he spoke in a loud voice, slowly pronouncing each word through clenched teeth. "You cussed at your teacher today."

"Well, a kid kept talking to me about the test we were taking, and the teacher kept telling me to be quiet." His voice trembled.

"I don't want to hear any of your damn excuses. Why did you swear at your teacher?"

"But, Dad, the other kid was the one doing the talking, and I just told him to shut up."

His dad clenched his fists. "Don't lie to me, you little shit. Do you really expect me to believe that story? It's always someone else's fault, isn't it?"

Johnny watched as his dad stomped across the room towards the kitchen. *Oh my God*, he thought. *He's getting a knife.* Then he spotted his walking stick. What was it doing in the kitchen? It had been in his bedroom that morning when he left for school. Then Johnny understood. His dad had wanted him to throw the stick away, but he had kept it, and now he was going to pay. What sweet revenge it would be for his dad to beat the holy shit out of him using the same stick he shouldn't have had in the first place.

As his dad picked it up, Johnny darted into the laundry room and shut the door. He couldn't quite get it closed, though. Then he looked down and saw the stick wedged into it. The adrenaline was pumping, and Johnny used every muscle in his scrawny thirteen-year-old body to hold the door shut. All the while, his dad was pushing and screaming at the top of his lungs.

Suddenly, he stopped pushing and yelled, "Open this door now, boy." Then, with all his weight, he pushed so hard that Johnny couldn't hold it any longer. The door flew open with his dad tumbling in and almost falling to the floor.

Johnny cowered in the corner, as his dad picked up the stick and started to hit him with a vengeance. Over and over he beat him as Johnny tried to ward off the blows by holding his hands and arms over his face. Finally, he squeezed down between the wall and the side of the washing machine, but that only served to leave his backside wide open for the attack.

The stick broke in several pieces, and his dad started jabbing him with what was left of it.

"Please stop, Dad," he sobbed. "You're going to kill me. Please, Dad. I'm sorry."

Mercifully, the jabbing stopped. His dad reached for the door and glared at him. "Now, throw the damned stick away," he said.

Johnny must have lain there for hours. With great difficulty, he picked up what was left of the stick. Then he went to his room and spent the rest of the week there. He came out only occasionally to eat and to use the bathroom. He was thankful the school suspended him, because he was so sore he could barely walk, let alone function as a student. He spent his hours picking slivers out of his arms and putting peroxide on his scratches.

He returned to school the following Monday, the same day he had gym class. That meant he would have to wear shorts. It had been a week since the beating, so if anything, he looked worse. Although the swelling had gone down, some of the purple and black bruises were taking on a deep yellowish green color. They covered his body from head to toe.

Johnny wished someone would ask him what happened. He wanted so badly to be able to tell that his dad beat the shit out of him. Surely, everyone must assume that he got beat at home, but the subject seemed to be taboo. No one—not students, not teachers—even asked him.

Johnny's thirteenth birthday was the day he left his childhood behind and crossed the threshold to the slow journey of becoming a man. But he didn't feel like a man just then. He felt like a prisoner.

NINE

On November 24, 1975, Jill turned fifteen, and Richard suddenly stopped molesting her.

He approached her one day and spoke as bluntly as ever. "You are going to move out of this house, or I am going to kick your ass every single day that you stay."

The choice was an easy one for Jill. She left.

Her boyfriend Daniel's* parents were very fond of her, and they let her move into one of their rental properties with their daughter Holly*. They even helped Jill move her possessions out of her parents' home. Janyce stood on the patio crying as she watched her leave. Still, Jill could tell that her mom was angry. She didn't even tell her goodbye. Jill left that house having no regrets.

Her first night away from home was the best she'd had in years. She felt that a huge weight had been lifted off of her. Just knowing that she never had to go back to that house again made her feel safe and happy.

She got a job at a fast-food restaurant and stayed with Holly until after she graduated from high school. Graduation was a big deal for Jill, but apparently not for her family. Not one of them attended the ceremonies. Jill's mom at least acknowledged the fact by sending her a watch with a note attached telling her to come and visit. It only made Jill cry. She just wanted her mom, not a cheap watch.

A short while after she graduated, she and Daniel moved into their own apartment. With the help of Daniel's parents, Jill was able to attend school to become a medical assistant. She also continued her fast-food job while Daniel finished his senior year.

* * *

Johnny was just finishing the seventh grade, and he had started witnessing his parents' wild behavior.

One day when his dad was sunbathing in the backyard, and Johnny was throwing around the football, his dad asked Linda, his older daughter, to grab the shoebox.

"Shoebox?" Johnny asked. "What for?"

"You'll see," his dad replied.

They sat down outside underneath the patio, and Linda came out with the shoebox.

She went over to Johnny and held it out.

"Do you know how to roll?" she asked.

"Roll what?" he joked. "Sure I do."

Richard had a rolling machine, papers, and of course, a stash of marijuana. He rolled one up, and the three of them sat in the backyard taking turns puffing away on the joint.

His dad sat in that lounge chair taking a big, big hit—then looking over at Johnny, kicking back, closing his eyes and blowing it out—he said, "Here ya go, Johnny. Take a hit. You'll enjoy it."

He enjoyed it, all right. From that day on, Johnny knew he was in trouble.

* * *

In the fall of 1976, Richard put his Playmates Unlimited red phone to work, and he became a fulltime bookie. His illegal gambling business was centered on bookmaking of sporting events, particularly college and professional football. Again, the money was flowing in.

In addition to his fulltime bookmaking career, Richard hosted a lot of card games at the family home on Locust. Gin rummy was his game of choice, and he was good at it. When he played with his Italian friends, including Johnny's Uncle Ted, they often played at the Regency Hotel in Denver, which Ted and his family had built. Sometimes they stayed there playing for days at a time.

One night when he was about fourteen, Johnny came home to

find his dad and a whole crowd at the house playing cards. One of the Italian guys called himself Big Billy. When Johnny's dad introduced him, Big Billy slowly got up out of his chair. As he did, he kept getting taller and taller. It was like looking up at the Jolly Green Giant. He seemed as tall as he was wide. When they shook hands, Big Billy's engulfed Johnny's. It was huge.

* * *

On December 11 of that year, the police arrested Richard at his home on Locust and charged him with operating an illegal gambling business in violation of the laws of Colorado and interstate use of a telephone to facilitate gambling business. Criminal charges were filed against him on June 30, 1977, and his arraignment was held on July 18, 1977.

Over the course of the following six months, Richard appeared at five different preliminary hearings. The jury trial was held on March 16, 1978. On April 14, 1978, Richard appeared once again for a deposition hearing/reset date, and sentence was entered. On October 17, 1978, he appeared for a final hearing, and the charges were dismissed, without prejudice by the court.

In 1976, Charles Smaldone, the boss of the Italian Mafia in Denver at the time, was arrested, along with eleven others, for operating an illegal gambling business. The indictment named twelve people as defendants, and the eight defendants convicted by the jury filed for an appeal.

The rehearing was denied on October 17, 1978, the same day the charges against Richard were dismissed, without prejudice. According to the court documents, the informant on the Smaldone case was never identified. Smaldone and five others were convicted of conspiring to violate the federal statute relating to interstate travel or transportation in aid of racketeering enterprises. The same six appellants and a seventh appellant were convicted under a second count of conducting a gambling business.

Richard had a lot of friends in his back pocket, but he must have had a few enemies as well. If he had to take a guess at who snitched on him, he would guess it was his brother-in-law, Ted. Richard owed him eight-hundred dollars on a bet Ted placed and Richard had never reimbursed. Besides that, Ted was probably still miffed at Richard for winning Ted's Model-T car from him in a game of gin rummy one night at the Regency.

The family learned years later that Ted had indeed tipped off the police about Richard's illegal gambling operation.

TEN

Whether they were dealing with tenants, attorneys, businessmen, friends and acquaintances at the country club, clients, or their customers at The Cannery, Richard and Janyce had always wanted to look their best. Vain to a fault, both of them went as far as to acquire false driver's licenses so that they could pass themselves off as six years younger then they actually were.

When the Denver Tech Center added an athletic club to its facilities, both Janyce and Richard were eager to join. Their membership would not only allow them to keep their bodies in shape, but would also give them the opportunity to meet future business associates. Rather than spending their time in the workout room, they enjoyed playing racquetball with each other and were both very good at the game.

One day in early 1977, Janyce planned on meeting up with Helen in the hot tub after she and Richard had finished playing. When she got there, Helen was already relaxing with a woman named Cindy and her sister. She told Janyce they were involved in the restaurant business, and they struck up a conversation.

She and Cindy seemed to click from the start. They arranged to meet at the club that following Friday to play racquetball together. Richard and Janyce went to the club as planned. He didn't seem to mind that he had lost his partner in the game, and Janyce was certain it was because he loved watching women. She could tell from the look on his face that Richard was having more fun watching them than if he had been playing. If Cindy thought it was a little odd that her friend's husband didn't take his eyes off them the entire time, she didn't let on.

After the game, she invited them to come to her restaurant that Saturday evening.

"I'll reserve a table for you and treat you to prime rib and our best bottle of champagne," she said. "It's the Colorado Gold Mine Company in Glendale. My husband Buck and I own it."

Richard quickly spoke up. "I know where it is. We've always wanted to go there but were too busy at The Cannery."

"Good then," Cindy replied. "I'll see both of you tomorrow night at 6:30."

As agreed, Richard and Janyce showed up the next evening for dinner. Cindy and Buck greeted them at the door. The women complimented each other on how beautiful they looked in something other than their workout clothes, and Cindy showed them to their table.

The waiter treated them like royalty, and they knew that such pampering could only have come from Cindy. When they were finished and getting ready to leave, she stopped by their table.

"Thank you both for coming. I hope you enjoyed yourselves," she said. "Please come back."

Richard and Janyce both chimed in thanking her for the wonderful meal and telling her how much they enjoyed the atmosphere.

"We'll definitely be back," Richard said. "I'm curious about a sandwich that you have on your menu. It's priced at $49.95. Not to be rude, but does anyone really order that?"

Cindy couldn't help but laugh. "Oh yeah, the Fool's Gold Loaf, with bacon, peanut butter and grape jelly. The King himself eats it."

When they realized that she was referring to Elvis Presley, they both sat there with dumbfounded expressions.

"You don't mean he comes here to eat it, do you?" Janyce asked.

Cindy just smiled. "Elvis has been here before. I think he actually sat in the same chair you're sitting in now."

"Cool," Richard said. "We had quite a few famous athletes and local celebrities come into The Cannery, but I'm pretty sure that Elvis wasn't one of them."

"Well, the next time he stops here, I'll give you a call so you can see for yourself," she told him. "Of course, he'll be incognito, but I'll know him. Now, back to your question about the sandwich. One night, a year ago last February, Buck and I got a request to make twenty-two of them and deliver them to the airport. It seems that Elvis and two of his police friends from Denver were at his home in Graceland. Apparently, they started talking about the Fool's Gold Loaf sandwich, and Elvis decided he wanted one."

She explained that the men drove to Memphis and boarded Elvis' private jet, the Lisa Marie, and made the two-hour trip to Denver.

"In the meantime, Buck and I prepared the sandwiches," she said. "We personally delivered them to the airport. We also included several bottles of champagne and Perrier. Hanging out with them is an experience we will never forget."

Janyce was impressed, and she could see that Richard was too. More than that, however, she felt that Cindy might be the best friend she'd ever had.

* * *

They continued to meet at the athletic club several times a week. As much as Janyce had liked playing with Richard, a new partner was a refreshing change of pace. Soon she and Cindy became dear friends. Janyce felt she could confide in her without being judged. She didn't hold anything back when telling Cindy about Richard's and her sex lives.

"He's promiscuous," she said. "He likes threesomes, and he doesn't care if they are male or female."

"And you go along with it?" Cindy asked.

"Not at first. I didn't want any part of his kinky sex. The first time I was drunk and he gave me some kind of drug that made me willing to do anything. Now, I guess I've come to accept it for the most part. It is kind of fun when there's another man. But I must admit I am terribly jealous of the women. Most of the time, I won't join in. Richard has always brought strange women into our bed. No matter where we are, he is always looking for some young thing to bring home."

"Wait a minute" Cindy said. "I know Richard's not bad looking, but why would they just willingly go with him?"

"He's a very powerful man with a lot of connections," she replied. "I don't know what he says to them, but I'm sure a lot of it is the promise of drugs and money."

In the few minutes while they changed in a locker room, Janyce told Cindy as much as possible. That was the only time and place that they were ever alone. If Richard went to the locker room, Janyce would have to stand nearby for him to come out. If she spent too long changing, Richard would get angry and wait outside the door. When they came out, he would let Cindy pass. Then, while walking beside Janyce, he would elbow her as hard as he could in the ribs. Janyce winced causing Cindy to turn around and look. Still Janyce tried to appear as if nothing had happened. She knew if she let on to Cindy what Richard did to her, she would get a beating when she got home.

Richard didn't have to worry about her telling anyone how abusive he was to her. She was so ashamed that she didn't want anyone to know, although she knew those close to her guessed. Terrified as she was of Richard, she was forced to live her life with him, for him, around him. Whatever the man wanted, it was his life, and she was along for the ride—regardless of how bumpy the road got.

There were nights Janyce would go to bed thinking only how much she hated him. She would promise herself that she would not give him the chance to abuse her or her children again. This would be the last time. She would not forgive him, under any circumstances, no matter what. But she knew better than to try to fool herself. She had an undying love for her husband that never seemed to wane, no matter what he did to her. By the time she woke the next morning, she had already forgiven him. Richard would be by her side insisting that he was sorry. He would tell her how much he loved her and that he would take her to Mexico for a week. Janyce would always forgive him; she could not help herself.

When she was younger, if she got in a squabble with someone, she would always be the one to apologize so the other person wouldn't feel bad.

"Mother, what is wrong with me?" she had asked her mom. "Why do I always have to be so darn nice?"

Her mom looked at her, with loving eyes. "Honey, it's not a fault to be nice. It's an attribute, Janny. That's what makes you so special."

Now, her mother's expression, although still loving, was full of sadness.

"I'm so worried about you, Janny," she would say.

And always, Janyce would hug her, and say, "I'm fine. Everything's fine."

* * *

The seventies were coming to an end. Life was going to get better, Janyce knew. She had just celebrated her forty-second birthday, and she'd already accomplished so much in her life. She wasn't naive. Without Richard, she wouldn't have made it this far. But, by the same token, she believed he wouldn't be in the position he was without her.

Sometimes she did more than her share. She worked hard maintaining the books for all their holdings and different properties. Both she and Richard put in months of planning and years of hard work to make The Cannery the success that it had been.

She looked forward to the eighties as a change for their marriage. They would be celebrating their ninth wedding anniversary in a few weeks. Their kids were almost all adults now. Richard and she were both getting older, and she felt it was time for them to start growing up. She was tired of the drugs and drinking to excess, the all-night card parties, and the whores. It was time to start making some long-term plans for their future. She didn't want to keep living day to day and spending money like it was water. Janyce resolved to make the upcoming eighties a turning point in their lives.

ELEVEN

In 1980, Richard purchased some land off Alameda between Peoria and Havana in Aurora, Colorado. The last few months he had been involved with developing the land and turning it into a subdivision. He envisioned upscale homes boasting lush green lawns and hedges. Porches and Mercedes would gleam from every driveway. Here on Cedar Avenue, he and Janyce would build their dream home.

They had been discussing the home for years, and now it would become a reality for them. A large two-story brick home, it had a swimming pool in the backyard. Although Janyce's sister Helen was a well-known professional interior designer, her tastes leaned more toward the traditional. Janyce wanted her home to reflect her style. So she designed it herself in a red-white-and-blue color scheme.

The floors were covered wall to wall with plush red carpet. The use of colorful, flowered and patterned, textured wallpaper, incorporated with the white and blue on the walls turned out perfectly. Janyce was thrilled. She felt it was definitely her.

When the house was completely decorated, she invited her sister to come over and critique the finished results. When Helen saw it, she couldn't conceal her reaction. She was absolutely appalled and proclaimed the combination of colors and patterns as ghastly. Janyce just laughed.

Richard, Janyce, Johnny, and David moved into the house. The second floor was large enough to have four bedrooms. Instead, there were two apartment-like bedrooms and two full baths. Patricia would later occupy one room, while the remaining area was for Richard and Janyce. Three quarters of the upstairs of the home was made up of the master suite. Much of the space was used for walk-in closets. It was Janyce's idea for Richard and her to each have a closet the size of a bedroom. They both loved expensive clothes. Each had exquisite taste—and their closets showed it. Janyce also had a passion for shoes, so the space was customized to house her collection of well over one hundred pairs.

Johnny, age seventeen, and David, age nineteen, each chose a room in the basement. It also housed a main living area and a large bathroom. Richard dubbed the basement, "the Opium Den," and rightfully so. Drugs were aplenty, and Johnny and David soon began hosting wild parties.

Wanting a new car to go with his new home, Richard bought a 1980 930i Turbo Porsche and had it shipped straight from Germany. Shiny black anthracite with a pearly gray tint, the Porsche had black leather interior and real wood. It was fly-on-the-shift, meaning one could change gears without engaging the clutch.

Johnny loved the car and fantasized often about driving it. One evening when his parents weren't home, he and his friend Seth* were just hanging out, when on a whim, Johnny decided he wanted to take his dad's car to get cigarettes.

"No way, dude," Seth said. "You're crazy. Your old man will kill you if he finds out. Let's just take my car."

Johnny couldn't resist. The car seemed to be calling his name. The keys were in the ignition. He jumped in and started it. The sound of the engine was unbelievable. Without hesitation, Seth followed suit and settled into the passenger seat.

Johnny took off driving down Cedar Avenue out of the subdivision. He pulled onto Alameda Avenue and let it rip. The Porsche was doing sixty before he got it out of first gear. About that time, the ferring came out automatically and lowered the car to the ground to make it more aerodynamic.

Johnny glanced over and watched the back of Seth's head hit the seat as he punched the car from first gear into second and felt the ferring pop up. It was an unbelievable feeling as they sped down the street.

They cruised around for almost an hour, and Johnny even let Seth have a brief turn at driving. Then he took the wheel knowing they had better get the car home before they got busted. He pulled it into the parking lot of the 7-11 store. Seth ran into get the smokes, while Johnny waited with the music blasting out. Oh yeah, Johnny thought, he was pretty hot stuff sitting in this cool car.

He was singing along to the music as he looked up to see Seth coming out of the 7-11. He suddenly stopped dead in his tracks and made a pointing gesture with his finger, mouthing something Johnny could not make out. Johnny turned the volume down on the radio as Seth mouthed the words again. Then it hit him, and he could feel his face turning red, as the heat crept upward from his neck. Perspiration beaded on his forehead, and he felt as if he were going to throw up as he realized what Seth was trying to tell him. He was mouthing the words, *"Your old man..."*

He turned his head slowly and saw his dad parked in the space beside him.

"Johnny. You get my f***ing hundred thousand dollar car home now, boy."

Then he backed out and peeled out, screeching the tires.

Johnny motioned for Seth, who was still standing in the same spot, to hurry up and get in the car.

Seth got in, obviously scared. "What are you going to do?"

"There ain't no way in hell I'm going home. He'll kill me, dude. He will literally beat the crap out of me until I'm dead."

"Just go home and face him," Seth said. "He'll catch you sooner or later."

"You know my old man. He nearly killed me before. I'm as good as dead."

"I'll go with you," Seth said. "Then it won't be so bad."

Johnny reluctantly agreed and drove home. As soon as he pulled the car into the garage, Seth said, "I'm out of here dude."

Then he jumped out, took off running, then jumped in to his own car and sped off.

That pissed Johnny off. He would never forgive the powder-puff little bastard for leaving him. Now, he had to go in and face his dad—alone.

Johnny had no choice but to muster up all the courage he had and go into the house. Once inside, he ran down the stairs to his bedroom, looking around for something he could use to defend himself. If he was going to die, he wasn't going down without a fight. His baseball bat was on the carpet next to the closet. Johnny grabbed it and went to the far corner of his room to wait. He was shaking so badly that he had to lean against his dresser for support.

There in the shadowy corner, scared out of his mind, he listened for the sound of his dad's footsteps on the stairs. Then he heard it; someone moving around. Johnny held his breath as he waited for his dad to enter his room and kill him. But the sound wasn't on the stairs. It was the sound of the garage door opening.

Johnny sneaked up the stairs, and looking out the window, he caught a glimpse of the Porsche's taillights as it sped away. He couldn't believe his luck. He wasn't dead meat—yet.

Johnny went back downstairs and stayed in his room the rest of the evening. He didn't sleep well, haunted by nightmares and jumping every time he heard an unfamiliar sound.

The next morning, he got up to go to the bathroom. As he walked out of his room, he saw his dad waiting for him at the top of the stairs. He wanted to turn and run, but he was frozen. He couldn't move, as his dad stared down at him.

Seconds seemed to turn to hours before his dad finally spoke. "Johnny, boy. What in the hell ever possessed you to take my car?"

Johnny just stood there. He was too scared to say anything.

Apparently, his dad didn't need an answer, because to Johnny's complete and utter amazement, the only thing he said was, "Don't you *ever* do that again, or else." Then he turned and walked away. As he did so, Johnny could have sworn he heard him snicker.

He knew his dad probably enjoyed watching him tremble in fear, or maybe something like this had happened to him as a teen and made him decide to give Johnny a break. Whatever the reason, he thought that was the luckiest day of his life. He had lived to tell about it. But he was still pissed at Seth for telling him that he would stand by him, and then just taking off.

TWELVE

Jill was petite with brown eyes, a beautiful smile, thick shoulder-length wavy hair, olive skin, and a flawless complexion. Outgoing and bubbly, she was fun to be around, loving and compassionate. To be in her company, no one could imagine how deeply her soul had been scarred. People said she reminded them of her mom, and that made her happy in a way very little did.

After six months of living with Daniel, she learned that he had been making plans to attend college in California, and he didn't want Jill to move there with him. She couldn't afford the apartment on her own and was forced to move. At the same time, Kathy, Richard's daughter, was looking for a roommate. So Jill moved in with her. Kathy's house was right around the corner from Janyce and Richard's on Cedar Avenue.

Even though Jill had not been living at home for the last five years, she still kept in touch with her family. She was almost twenty now, and she hoped she could start to renew a relationship with her mom. She stopped over to see Janyce on occasion but was always careful to avoid Richard. The last thing she wanted was to be caught alone with him.

One evening while attending a party at her mom's house, Jill met one of the neighbors. His name was Clark*. He, his mother, and grandparents had recently moved in next door to Janyce and Richard's house. Jill was attracted to him the moment she saw him, and thought he looked like a Greek god with his dark hair and green eyes.

It wasn't long until they became a couple. Clark's mother and his grandparents were fond of Jill, and they all enjoyed spending time together, even though they were Greek and spoke very little English.

After they dated for almost a year, Clark moved in with Jill at Kathy's house. His family was very much against the arrangement and quickly decided that Jill was a slut. Clark's grandmother went so far as to put a curse on her. Soon after that, Clark became physically abusive, and Jill knew she didn't want to be another version of her mother.

One night Richard and Janyce invited them over to their house. Once there, they were invited to take a seat at the round glass-top table where Richard introduced them to cocaine. Jill wasn't afraid to try it. As they sat around the table, Richard explained how he had become friends with a doctor who introduced him to cocaine. At the time, the doctor swore to Richard that it wasn't addictive. Therefore it was the perfect drug. Richard even gave Jill a book praising its benefits.

She had heard that he was obsessed with going to the dentist. Now she knew why. That's where he got all his drugs. His dentist was the dealer. Richard wanted Clark and her to start selling drugs for him, and they made the deal. Richard would buy the cocaine, cut it and give it to them. In turn, they would sell it. Clark and Jill both did this for a while until they decided to cut Richard out of the deal, realizing it would be more profitable without him. After all, they knew who the dealer was. They would buy it directly from him.

Clark and Jill moved into their own townhouse, where they started seriously dealing. It was like open house with people coming in and out at all hours, but the couple didn't care. They didn't sleep. They didn't eat. They were on a cocaine high almost all the time. They held contests to see who could snort the most up one nostril. Jill usually won. She could snort almost a whole gram.

The drug dealing was getting bigger and bigger for them. Clark was working for a major airline company as a ramp agent at the international airport in Denver. He had the opportunity to fly to different countries, such as Peru and Bolivia, where he would purchase the cocaine. He smuggled it back into the states by either taping it to his waist or around his ankles.

While he was out of town, Jill worked at a doctor's office as a medical assistant. The couple never went to work high, but when they got home, it was party time. They had lots of friends, and everyone loved them.

As the months passed, Jill started to realize that she couldn't go on like this much longer. She wasn't really happy anymore. She weighed only ninety-seven pounds. If things kept up the way they were, she would end up either dead or in jail. People were getting busted all over, and she realized that if she didn't do something about it, she could be next.

One night she was with her girlfriend. Clark was out of town with her friend's husband, Adam*. Clark had prearranged a meeting to sell a few ounces of cocaine to a couple of guys he had met previously. When the guys called, Jill told them to come over to the house. She had never before involved herself in actually selling the drug, so she didn't know where Clark kept it. The guys were on their way. She and her friend were looking all over the house. Finally, she called Clark, who told her it was at Adam's house. In the meantime, the two guys showed up. Jill told them to just stay at the townhouse while she and her friend went to get the drugs. They got the cocaine and returned several minutes later. Jill made the sale. The guys turned out to be narks. Unwittingly, she had given them full access to the townhouse for at least ten minutes. She and her friend were lucky they weren't arrested. But the narks didn't want them. They wanted Clark. That was the last straw. Jill knew she had to get out of Denver. She called her friend in Phoenix to see if she could live with her. Her friend agreed, and Jill moved there shortly thereafter.

She stayed in touch with her girlfriend back in Denver, who was now going out with Clark. In one conversation, Jill learned that he had ended up in the hospital and almost died from an overdose. His drug count was higher than his blood count. A few months later, Jill was watching *America's Ten Most Wanted* and could have sworn it was Clark who was featured on the show. She also heard from her friend that he was under surveillance and had fled the country.

THIRTEEN

Johnny was still living at home with his parents on Cedar Avenue. He was eighteen years old now and a senior at Gateway High School. An average student, he received a lot of B's and C's. He planned on attending college in the fall, so during the week, he did the best he could to keep his grades up. The weekend was a different story. When Friday night rolled around, Johnny's brain seemed to do a 180. He quickly abandoned all thoughts of school. All he could think about was drugs, sex, and rock-n-roll.

Still he kept in touch with his best friends from his previous school, Seth, Kevin* and Matt*. They often came over to visit him on the weekends to party in the Opium Den. The basement was filled with smoke, beer, marijuana, x-rated movies, and sometimes girls. His parents were out partying every weekend at the local hot spots, so Johnny often had the house to himself. Even if his dad and mom did come home, they didn't care what he was doing. In fact, his dad usually joined them.

Sometimes he would get his dad's cocaine or marijuana out of his hiding place and share it with his friends. He had found out about it when his dad came home drunk one night and went for his stash. He watched as his dad retrieved it from inside the vent in the bathroom. From then on, Johnny had access to it whenever he wanted. His dad was so wasted most of the time that he never knew if any was missing. Johnny also discovered that he would sometimes hide his cocaine in a file cabinet in his office. He kept it in a folder filed under C. *If I had filed it for him, I would have put it in the D's for dumb-ass,* he thought.

One afternoon, Johnny invited Matt and Kevin to come over. They were sitting in the kitchen around the table. The glass table top functioned perfectly for cutting lines of cocaine.

His dad came into the room carrying a fast food hamburger box. Setting the box on the table, he asked, "Is anyone hungry?"

"Well, yeah, Dad," Johnny said, "but you only have one burger."

His dad sat down at the table and pushed the box over to Johnny.

"Open it," he said, "and then tell me that."

Johnny opened the box. Then he and his two friends stared wide-eyed at the contents. It was a rock of cocaine.

Through clenched teeth, Richard said, "Cut us up a few lines, Johnny."

This wasn't anything new. Johnny had observed his dad doing it several times before. Besides, he had perfected the skill on his own, and he gladly obliged. They all took turns snorting the lines. Johnny thought his dad was so cool to share his coke and get high with him and his friends. Maybe they could really be close now.

* * *

By August of 1982, Richard and Janyce were well-known for their over-the-top parties. Johnny was just shy of turning twenty. His mom made all the plans for a summer party. It was held in the backyard by the pool. A dance floor was set up along with seating for about fifty people. It seemed the whole family was there, including Jill, Patricia, Uncle Ted, Auntie Helen, Nanny and Poppy, Grandpa and Grandma Bloom, his cousin Brenda, and her boyfriend Kurt*. His mom booked a belly dancer, juggler, DJ, and two live tigers. There was plenty of hard liquor, wine, and champagne, which was kept in the garage.

Johnny and Seth took care of the valet duties and parked all the cars. The boys set up shop in the garage and had a neat system worked out between them. Johnny's dad was still in the process of developing the subdivision that surrounded their home on Cedar Avenue. There were still empty lots, and the street was empty, so there was plenty of room for parking. Or so Johnny thought until he started drinking.

The neat system somehow failed after Johnny had drunk too much. He was parking some guy's Corvette in the lot when he backed up too far and hit a car. Johnny kept backing, and then, in his drunken stupidity, hit the gas and floored it, hitting the same car again.

His dad smoothed everything over with the Corvette owner and promised to pay for the damages. Needless to say, Johnny was in big trouble once again.

He and Seth took a break and went into the back to see the tiger. The trainer had two of them and brought them out of his truck one at a time. He kept the first one on a long, heavy, link chain as he led him into the backyard. Some people hung back unsure, while others wanted to touch him. All of a sudden, the tiger must have wanted to cool off, because he jumped into the pool. The trainer let him swim around for a few minutes before pulling him out.

"Could you get us a drink of water?" he asked Janyce.

She went to the kitchen and came back carrying a huge glass salad bowl filled with water. For some reason the tiger freaked out and slapped the bowl. It went flying and twirled through the air until it came back down crashing onto the patio and breaking into a million pieces. That caused frenzy among the guests. The tiger approached a woman who was standing nearby and started clawing at her leg. The trainer was lucky that the tiger didn't rip her leg off. He decided it was time to take his pets home.

That little incident didn't deter the party goers. Something was going on in every room of the house. Johnny's dad even had a special room set up downstairs in his Opium Den, which was dimly lit and furnished with comfortable furniture and big throw pillows. A coffee table in front of the sofa held an assortment of drugs and paraphernalia. All of the televisions throughout the house were set up playing porn films. It seemed like no one wanted to go home. The party continued throughout the night and into the early morning hours.

FOURTEEN

It was November 13, 1983, a couple of weeks before Thanksgiving. The night began much like any other evening for Janyce and Richard. They went out for dinner at the El Torrito Restaurant, where they started drinking. But on this particular night, instead of driving home, they decided to stay at The Denver Marriott Hotel SE. It was only a couple of blocks away, so they left their car where it was parked and walked to the hotel. Richard checked the two of them into Room 335. They barely got settled into their room before he was on the phone ordering a bottle of their best champagne from room service.

Janyce had no way of knowing that he'd had sex with men over the years. Although he didn't think of himself as gay, he enjoyed frequenting Empire Baths downtown and discovered he had a passion for anal sex. Tonight he was going to introduce his wife to it.

Janyce had gone along with almost all of Richard's sexual fantasies—everything from threesomes to wild orgies—for fear of displeasing him. But she had never wanted to engage in anal sex. They sat around talking and having a few more glasses of champagne, and then got into bed and began making love. While they were having sex, Richard told her how he fantasized about having anal sex with her and with another man in their bed at the same time. He told her about his sexual experiences at the bathhouse and how it had almost become an addiction for him. He wanted Janyce to experience the same pleasures he had.

He turned her over onto her stomach.

"No," she screamed. "I'm not going to let you do this. Just get off me and let me sleep."

Richard, enraged, got out of bed and grabbed his cowboy boot. He walked back to where she was still lying on her stomach.

"I'll teach you never to disobey me, you bitch." He lifted his boot and started beating Janyce. It took her a second before she realized what was happening—Richard must be hitting her with something hard. She was thinking: *Oh dear God—help me—what have I done?*

Richard continued striking her on her head and back, over and over again. He pushed her head into the pillow to stifle her screams for help. She tried to roll over, but he kept hitting her. Then he tore the lamp off the wall next to the bed and began striking her with it. Janyce felt something warm running down from her head, onto her face and mouth. She realized it was blood. She could see it pooling onto the hotel's white sheets and spreading as she struggled to move.

Richard dropped the lamp and went into the bathroom. He got into the shower and yelled at Janyce, "Get your ass up and get in here now."

None of the beatings she'd endured over the years was as severe as this one. She felt that if she didn't get away this time, he would kill her. She mustered what strength she had left and bolted out the door. Then she ran down the long hallway, naked and bleeding from head to toe. It played in her head like a scary movie. The hallway seemed to go on forever. And if she looked back, she knew he would be there ready to grab her.

Finally she reached the elevator. The doors wouldn't open. The elevator was in use. She kept hitting the down button, feeling her heart pounding in her chest. She was overwhelmed with a sense of fear that Richard was going to grab her at any second.

It seemed like hours before the doors opened. When they did, there were two men and a woman standing inside. All three gasped in horror when they saw Janyce standing there naked and bloody. One of the men took off his jacket and put it around her.

As the elevator doors were closing, she heard Richard yelling, "Get your ass back in the room."

The three people helped Janyce through the lobby and to the front desk, where the night clerk phoned the police. The clerk then helped her to a small room behind the desk area. She was still bleeding profusely from her head injuries. Her tears made clean white lines starting at her eyes and running down her cheeks as they ran through the blood on her face. Her dark matted hair hung in sticky globs around her shoulders. She clung to one side of the jacket, as she tried to cover her nakedness. Her other arm hung limply at her side. She was shaking uncontrollably.

"I'm so sorry," the clerk said. "What kind of a man would do this? I'm going to call an ambulance."

"No," Janyce pleaded. "Just call me a taxi. I have to get to my home as quickly as possible. I can get help later."

At that moment, a female employee came into the room to see if she could help. When she saw Janyce, she had to hold back a scream. She heard that a woman was beaten, but this was far worse than she had imagined. She tried to compose herself as she entered the room. She didn't want the look on her face to reveal how scared she was for the woman. She walked over to Janyce and introduced herself as Gail*. Gail said she would help her clean herself up, while Janyce waited for the taxi.

In the bathroom, she had Janyce sit on the toilet seat. Gail grabbed a towel and started wiping the blood off her face. She was being as careful as she could, because she couldn't tell exactly what injuries the woman had. There was blood coming from everywhere, and it wouldn't stop. Gail put the towel on Janyce's head and instructed her to hold it there.

"Sit tight, honey," she said. "I'll be right back." She ran to the storage closet in the adjoining room.

When she returned, she was carrying an ace bandage and a lightweight blanket. She sure wasn't a nurse, but she knew she had to try to stop the bleeding. She didn't know if the woman was cold, scared, or in shock, but she was shaking like a leaf. Gail covered her with the blanket, and Janyce winced in pain when the clerk touched her arm.

"I think my arm is broken," she said. "It really hurts, and I can hardly move it."

"What happened?" Gail asked. "Did someone rape you, or what?"

"It was my son-of-a-bitch husband," Janyce replied. "He gets drunk, and then beats the hell out of me. It's like a game for him, but this is the last time."

61

Gail could tell that the woman was intoxicated, but she hoped she meant what she said. Judging from her appearance, she was married to one mean SOB.

Gail wrapped the bandage around Janyce's head. The blood was starting to show through the bandage, but that was the best she could do under the circumstances. Then Janyce asked Gail if she would go up to their hotel room and get her clothes and purse.

At that moment, a police officer came into the room and asked Janyce to tell him what happened. She told the officer everything.

"Want to press charges?" he asked.

Janyce almost broke out into laughter, thinking to herself, *Yeah right. You don't know my husband very well. He has friends in high places, and they are all assholes, just like him. One's his cousin, who is a lieutenant with the police department right here in Denver, and others have ties to the Italian and Jewish mafias.* She kept her thoughts to herself, and said that she didn't want to have Richard arrested.

"Could you at least hold him long enough for me to go home so I can get a few things together and find a place to stay?" she asked.

"I'll try," he said and left the room.

In the meantime, another policeman escorted Gail up to the hotel room to retrieve Janyce's things. As they entered the room, Gail was shocked by the bloody bed, not to mention the trail of blood from the bed to the door. The policeman helped Gail locate Janyce's purse, clothing, shoes, and coat. As Gail was leaving the room with the policeman at her side, she couldn't help but steal a sideways glance at the man the other two police officers were questioning. As she looked over at him, their eyes met. She realized that he had been staring at her. Gail looked away as quickly as she could. But it wasn't quick enough. She would never forget the look on his face. The guy was downright creepy. She couldn't wait to get out of that room.

Gail returned with Janyce's belongings. She helped her get her dress and shoes on, and was only able to put the coat around Janyce's shoulders, because of her injured arm. Then she helped Janyce through the empty lobby out to the street, where the taxi was waiting.

FIFTEEN

The cab driver pulled into the circular drive at the Hansens' residence on East Cedar Avenue about 1:30 A.M. The house was dark, and it appeared as if no one was home. Janyce noticed a car parked out front. Her heart began to beat faster, and panic started to set in. Then she realized the car belonged to Nancy, her live-in maid for about a year now. She had taken Johnny's bedroom when he left for college. At about the same time, David had moved out and in with his new girlfriend.

Janyce paid the driver. He got out and helped her to the front door.

"Can I do anything else for you?" he asked.

"I'm fine," she replied, although she'd never been in more pain. "My maid is home. She can help me."

Janyce went in and turned on the lights.

"Nancy," she called.

The maid quickly got up. She was used to these late-night disturbances, and she frequently woke to the sound of Richard and Janyce yelling at each other. Sometimes, it escalated into more than a yelling match. There were many nights when the two came home drunk and screaming, and Nancy could hear the clatter and crash of furniture being knocked around. Jill had warned her how violent Richard could get. She had said that it was best not to try and help, because it would only make things worse, and Richard would come after her.

Still, Nancy could not ignore Janyce's cry. She hurried into the room, and when she saw her, she began to cry.

"He did this to you, didn't he?" She didn't wait for an answer. Instead, she went into action, locking the doors, certain that Richard would come charging in any second.

Give me a minute to get dressed, and I'll take you to the emergency room," she told Janyce. "We need to hurry and get out of here."

"Don't worry," Janyce said. "The police are detaining him at the hotel. I need you to help me pack a few of my things and then get me out of here."

As Nancy helped her up the stairs to the master bedroom, she was shocked at how frail she felt. *My God. She must be running on pure adrenaline. By the looks of her, she should be dead.* They made it up to the bedroom.

"Get my overnight bag," Janyce said then pointed to a suitcase on the closet shelf. "That one too."

Nancy pulled the suitcase off the shelf, placed it on the bed, and opened it. Then she gasped. Before her were hundreds and hundreds of dollars. Nancy gawked at the sight of all that cash as Janyce took a few handfuls and shoved the bills into her bag.

"Get as many of my clothes as you can fit in," she said. "Then get my personal items and makeup bag out of the bathroom."

As Nancy followed her instruction, Janyce started to leave the room, and then something caught her eye. She was startled for a moment. Then realized she was looking at her own reflection in the mirror. What a pitiful sight. She looked at the woman, head bandaged, shoulder-length dark hair matted and sticking all over her face.

What happened to make her life go so wrong when everything was so right in the beginning? She had been so deeply hurt—mentally, as well as physically. But she couldn't take the time to feel sorry for herself now. She knew she had to stay mad, or he would sweet talk his way back into her life. She needed to get out of here before Richard came home. She wanted him out of her life for good.

Nancy helped Janyce down the stairs and told her to wait in the house while she took the bags out to her car. It was a cold November night, so Nancy wanted to start the car and warm it up. She soon returned, and helped Janyce into the car.

Although she wanted to take her to the emergency room, Janyce said no. She told Nancy to take her to Janyce's parents' house ten minutes away. She had been there before with Jill, so she knew the way. As she drove the car out of the driveway, she said, "Put your head back and try to get some rest. You're going to be okay now."

During the drive, Nancy mentally replayed getting the suitcase down from the shelf and opening it. She couldn't get over all that money. There must be a million dollars in there. She always figured that the Hansens had money, but she also had her suspicions that something shady was going on. She couldn't quite put her finger on it.

Richard hosted a lot of card games. He and his friends would sit at the kitchen table and play gin rummy for two or three days at a time. They kind of reminded her of a mob or something. When he had them over, she pretty much stayed in her room or left the house. The less she knew about what went on, the better off she would be.

As they approached the home, Nancy reached over and gently shook Janyce. In the driveway, she let the car idle as she retrieved the overnight bag out of the back seat, and then went around to the passenger side to help Janyce out of the car.

"Thank you," Janyce said. "You can go now."

"But you can hardly stand. I want to stay with you."

"I'll be okay," she insisted. "Just go. I don't want to argue with you."

Reluctantly, she agreed. "I'll be staying over at my friend's house if you need me for anything," she said. "I am not going to risk running into Richard. Take care of yourself."

Janyce's father opened the door, took one look at her, then yelled, "Molly, come here. Hurry."

Janyce looked up at him, sobbing. "Daddy, it was Richard," she said, and then collapsed in a heap at the doorstep.

He reached down, scooped her up, then carried her in and laid her on the couch. Her mother rushed into the room, and when she saw Janyce, started crying.

"Oh, dear God. What happened? Dear Lord. Ben. What happened to our Janny?"

"What the hell do you think? It was that god dam, no good, son-of-a-bitch, Richard."

Molly gently wrapped her arms around her daughter and held her while Ben called the family physician. Their doctor told them to take her to the emergency room immediately and said he would meet them there.

They drove her there and stayed with her while the doctors checked her over. Her beating had left her with sixty-eight stitches to her head alone. Her arm was broken, and she had numerous bruises and cuts from head to toe.

As they drove away from the hospital, it was almost dawn. Janyce went home with her mom and dad. They tried to get a couple hours of sleep but found themselves waking to every sound, terrified that Richard was coming for their Janny.

But he would not have posed a problem for them that evening. He was in jail. Although Janyce didn't want him arrested, the manager at The Denver Marriott Hotel SE did. Someone had to be held accountable for the lamp that was pulled from the wall, as well as the bloody linens and mattress. Richard was arrested in the hotel at 1:20 A.M. and received a summons for destruction of property in room #335--lamp torn from the wall $75.00; bloody sheets, mattress and bedding.

As intimidating as he was, Richard couldn't talk his way out of this one. When the two officers arrested him, he threatened to have his connection at the Denver Police Department *beat the f**** out of them. This statement is handwritten on the back of the officer's copy of the summons (including the name of Richard's connection). After staying in jail overnight, his bond was posted, and he was released the next morning.

* * *

Molly and Ben decided it wasn't safe for Janyce in Denver, so they made plans for her to go to Arizona to stay with her sister, Helen, who was with her husband at their winter home in Scottsdale.

Because Janyce wanted to be the one to tell her sister what happened, her mother called Helen and said Janny and Richard were having problems, and Janny needed some time away from him to work things out.

Helen was delighted, as she considered Janyce her best friend, and Richard always made it impossible for them to spend time together. She began making mental plans for all of the things they could do together, and she could hardly wait for her sister to arrive.

* * *

Janyce caught the next flight out of Denver to Phoenix. Helen picked her up at the airport and was horrified by her appearance. She had never seen Janyce anything but fashionable. Now, her sister was dressed in ill-fitting clothes. A scarf covered her hair, and her arm was in a cast. Helen assumed that Richard was at fault. She would have to wait until they reached her house before she would find out.

They made small talk on the drive, and when they arrived at her house, Janyce explained what had happened at the hotel. Then she took off her scarf. Helen's first thought was that she had gotten a bad haircut. A closer look told a much different story. A large section of hair on the back of her head had been shaved. There were jagged lines resembling train tracks going every which way. What hair she did have was matted with dried blood.

"Although Mom helped me wash my hair before I left for the airport, it was almost impossible because of the stitches," she said, "and she had to cut at least four inches off the rest of it. I look terrible, I know."

Helen was so choked up she couldn't speak. She hugged Janyce as gently as she could, and they cried together.

Janyce felt so ashamed. She had never wanted anyone to know that Richard physically abused her. Although the family had their suspicions, she managed to keep most of it a secret. It had been easy to cover up or explain away the bruises before. She would hide her injuries by wearing long sleeves, by applying a little extra makeup, or she'd just say she ran into something. He was usually careful not to leave any telltale signs on her face. She had never even confided in her best friend, Cindy, about the physical abuse. Richard said he would kill her if she ever told anyone. Well, now she had.

SIXTEEN

November 14, 1983. Jill was living with Richard and Janyce again at their home on Cedar Avenue in the spare bedroom upstairs. However, she had been out of town for a few days, and was shocked to receive a call from Nancy explaining what had happened and how severely Richard had beaten Janyce. Jill made arrangements for Nancy to pick her up at the airport when she arrived back in Denver. It was about 6:00 p.m. the following evening when the plane landed. Jill reached overhead and retrieved her carry-on bag. She exited the plane and quickly made it through the airport to where Nancy was waiting outside.

"Thanks so much," she said and got in the car.

"It's no problem," Nancy told her. "I haven't had much to do lately. You could say I don't have a job. I'm not going to work at your mom's house until she comes home. It's too creepy being in there with your dad."

"Please don't ever call him my dad," Jill said. "The fact that he adopted me doesn't mean a thing."

"Is your mom going to come home?" Nancy asked. "I wouldn't if my husband beat me up like that."

Jill sighed. "She will eventually. She always does. He won't give her any other choice. This discussion is creeping me out. Do you want to spend the night at my house?"

"I can't," Nancy replied. "I promised my friend that I would go with her in the morning."

Jill assumed that was just an excuse so Nancy wouldn't have to come over. But she couldn't blame her. She didn't want to go home herself.

Nancy pulled into the circular drive and dropped Jill off at the front door. The house was dark. Richard didn't appear to be home. They said their goodbyes, and Nancy left.

As Jill entered the house, she silently thanked God that Richard wasn't there. She dreaded the thought of being in the house alone with him. It was especially frightening without her mom there. When Richard did come home, she couldn't imagine the state of mind he would be in with his wife being gone. He was used to having control over everything and everyone around him. But now, he seemed to have lost control over his wife, at least for the time being.

Jill hurried to unpack and put her things away. She was hoping he would be so drunk he wouldn't realize she was there. She would make sure to leave everything as it was, even her bedroom door half open. If she shut it, he might guess that she was home.

He was so disgusting that she couldn't stand being in the same room with him. It didn't matter if there were other people around or not. He would always come up with some sort of sexual innuendo directed toward her. He would look around to make sure no one was watching, and then he would leer at her and put his finger in his mouth and suck on it, trying to imply something sexual. It had been over seven years since the last time he had sexually molested her. She thought maybe he stopped because he was afraid she would get pregnant. Still, she was terrified every night thinking he would come in to her bed. She was fifteen when it ended, but in Jill's mind, it was as if it had happened yesterday.

She got into bed, turned off the lights, and pulled the covers up to her neck. Soon, all of the familiar feelings of insecurity began to well up in her. No matter how hard she tried to push the bad feelings away, they always came to her when she went to bed. Fear crept up and enveloped her like the darkness. It clung to her and stayed the night. Not until she saw the morning light would she feel somewhat safe again.

As she lay there praying for sleep to come, she started to cry. The memories of what happened eleven years ago slowly crept into her head. It was the first time that Richard came to her bed. Jill remembered the little girl who was only ten years old. She was so scared. He had hurt her so badly, and no one ever came to help.

Suddenly, a familiar noise startled her. It was the sound of the front door opening. Then she heard someone shuffling across the floor towards the stairway. Jill's room was up the stairs and the last room on the left. Her bed was angled so she could see out into the hallway. As she watched and listened, she soon made out the shadow of a man. For a split second, she wished that it would be an intruder, anyone but Richard. But she could see the dark figure was that of her so-called father.

He topped the stairs and went into his room, and Jill slowly turned to face the wall. She lay there as still as possible, assuring herself that the danger had passed. But soon she heard Richard stumbling down the hall toward her room. She wondered if he had been checking every night to see if she was in bed or not. She thought about hiding in the closet or even under the bed. But she knew he would find her and be madder than ever. Then he would make her sorry.

He entered the bedroom and crossed to her bed. Jill's whole body stiffened. She tried not to breathe as she lay there terrified. He pulled the covers down and got into bed with her. She clenched her mouth shut to keep from gagging. Although her back was to him, he reeked. The familiar smell of Old Spice mixed with liquor was enough to make her vomit. She felt his naked body press against her back, as he put his arm around her.

"Get out," she yelled and tried to push him away.

"Can't a father hug his daughter?" he slurred.

As Jill struggled to get away, her fear was turning into anger. There was no stopping the profanity that came out of her mouth.

"Get the f*** off of me, you perverted son-of-a-bitch." She turned pushing and kicking him as hard as she could, screaming. "Not now, and not ever again, will you ever touch me, you drunken bastard."

He landed on the floor, and as she was trying to figure out what to do next, he pulled himself up and left the room. Surprised, Jill ran to the door, slammed it shut and locked it.

Hammering came from the other side. He was pounding on it. "Open the door, you bitch. Open it now, whore, or I'll kill you."

Almost frozen with fear, heart pounding, Jill backed away from the door. She inched her way toward the window, where she removed the screen. Her room was on the second floor. She was prepared to jump out the window if he got into the room.

Abruptly, the pounding and yelling stopped. Richard had apparently given up on getting in and gone back to his room to pass out. Eventually, Jill got back into her bed, pulling the covers securely around her neck. After lying there for what seemed like hours, she allowed herself to fall asleep.

As the morning light entered her room, she felt a little less afraid. She quickly packed an overnight bag and drove over to her boyfriend's house. When she arrived, she told Gary* what had happened between her mom and Richard. She also explained that her mom had told Nancy not to tell anyone about the beating. This time Jill couldn't ignore what had happened. She needed to see for herself that her mom was all right. Gary drove her straight to the airport and bought Jill a ticket to Arizona. She was on the next flight out, still smelling Richard's foul odor, still hearing his threats *"I'll kill you."*

* * *

When she saw her mom for the first time since the beating, Jill's reaction was much the same as Helen's. As horrified as she was by the bruises, stitches and broken arm, more than anything, she was angry. She had never hated Richard this much, and she was terrified of her mom returning to him.

The few days at her Auntie Helen's went by fast. Jill would have liked to stay longer to help her mom, but she had to get back to work. Besides, her mom wanted her to do a little investigating at home. She wanted Jill to see if Richard was up to no good. Not that she gave a damn, Janyce just wanted to make sure he wasn't making plans for her to return home.

A few days later, Richard began calling for Janyce at Helen's. It wasn't too difficult to find out where she was staying. The first few times Helen or Ted put him off by saying Janyce wasn't able to come to the phone, or she was sleeping. Helen told Richard any excuse she could think of to keep her sister from having to talk to him. Sometimes he would call four or five times a day, at all hours of the day and night. Every time the phone would ring, Janyce got a queasy feeling in her stomach.

She knew he would keep calling until she talked to him. She also knew he would never let her go. He would possess every inch of her body and soul until the day she died.

Finally she decided to talk to him. She listened to all his promises again. She knew them all by heart because she had heard them all many times before. He would quit drinking. He would quit doing drugs. He insisted that he would never lay a hand on her again. His addictions were what made him hurt her. He loved her more than anything in the world, and he couldn't live without her. She knew if she didn't give in, his kindness would soon turn to threats, and then they would all have to pay.

Helen and Ted begged her not to go back to him. Ted said he had exposure to all kinds of people—good and bad—but Richard was one of the scariest men he had ever known. Not because of the way he looked, but rather because of the way he lived his life. His scruples, his temper, his total disregard of other people, and his low morals were unfathomable, Ted said. Over the past ten years, he had watched Richard do his best to destroy everyone around him.

Ted and Helen continued to plead, but Janyce insisted that she still wanted to make her marriage work.

"One day, he'll kill you," Ted said.

* * *

A few days before Richard beat up Janyce, he was made aware of a certain transaction involving property in which he owned an interest. The transaction, made without his knowledge, resulted in the loss of thousands of dollars to him. He learned of this in a phone conversation he had with Ted. Both Ted and Helen thought that he had taken out his anger on Janyce to get back at them, because he knew the three of them were so close.

In 1970, Richard, Ted, and Ted's brother, Victor, had formed a partnership in order to purchase and operate the Thunderbird Apartments in Boulder, Colorado. Richard managed the daily operations and the apartments until 1977, when a dispute arose among the partners regarding his management and accounting. The three settled the dispute in an agreement, whereby Victor purchased Richard's interest in the partnership based on a value for the apartments of $725,000. The closing took place on November 15, 1977.

Unbeknownst to Richard, on the same day he sold his share to Victor, Ted and Victor contracted with and sold the building to the new buyer for $825,000. Apparently, the brothers had been in contact with the buyer at least four times in the three months preceding the sale. The closing took place on January 3, 1978.

Sometime in 1978, Richard learned about the sale of the apartments. Since he wasn't aware of the terms of the sale or the brothers' prior negotiations with the buyer, at the time, the news was of no consequence to him.

Now, here it was five years later, and Ted was telling him all about how they sold the apartment building to an interested buyer. He rubbed in the fact, adding that they laughed all the way to the bank. Richard ended the conversation and immediately called the buyer, who confirmed everything Ted had told him. Richard wasn't about to let his brother-in-law or Victor get away with ripping him off.

He sent Victor a letter claiming he breached his fiduciary duty by not disclosing the negotiations with the buyer. He demanded his share of one hundred thousand, which was the difference between the settlement price and the price the buyer paid for the apartment building. Shortly thereafter, he received a reply from Victor's attorney acknowledging receipt of the letter and stating he would have his response shortly.

Tired of waiting, Richard filed a lawsuit against Victor Lederman on February 9, 1984. He won in court and was awarded compensatory damages in the amount of $33,333.33, and punitive damages in the amount of three thousand. The trial court would later hold a hearing on Richard's claim for prejudgment interest and award him $52,502.95 in interest from November 15, 1977 through the date of trial, July 3, 1985. Victor would later appeal the court's decision on April 7, 1988. The Colorado Court of Appeals found Victor's assignments of error to be without merit and upheld the trial court's decision, and judgment was affirmed in his favor.

* * *

After two weeks in Scottsdale, Janyce returned home and reunited with Richard. She set the rules in place for both of them, a new way of life. She insisted that it was time for both of them to grow up. It was the only way they could leave the bad times behind and look ahead to the future. She longed for a happy home where her children and grandchildren would always be welcome.

Janyce admitted that she was no saint, and she took responsibility for her own actions. In the past, her intentions had always been good when she discussed wanting to change, but the changes never lasted long. This time was going to be it, and if it wasn't, she would go to the ends of the earth to keep Richard out of her life forever. The first thing that they had to do was quit drinking. Absolutely no alcohol would be allowed in the house, and certainly no drugs.

SEVENTEEN

On September 21, 1984, a call came into the Aurora Police Department as a possible suicide. Officers were dispatched to 12754 East Cedar Avenue.

First responders arriving at approximately 2:53 a.m. included a rescue unit and fire engine from the Aurora Fire Department. Shortly thereafter, several officers from the Aurora Police Department arrived.

Among the first on the scene were Officers E. J. Hockom, Timothy Huffman, and J. Turner. As Officer Hockom approached, he noticed a man and young woman standing in the driveway. The two were later identified as Richard Hansen, the owner of the house, and his twenty-two year old daughter, Patricia Hansen. Richard was wearing dark trousers and a white shirt, and Patricia was wearing a pink bathrobe.

Richard was shouting and crying, "She's dead. She's dead, isn't she?" He was extremely hysterical, pacing around and waving his arms wildly, banging on a brick wall in front of the house. Then he began pulling out pieces of vines from the landscaping and throwing them to the ground, screaming, "She's dead, she's dead. She was waiting in the car for me."

His daughter stood on the front lawn crying as she watched him.

After observing the man's behavior Officer Hockom walked over to the open garage door where he was met by an overwhelming smell of exhaust fumes. The home had a two-car attached garage. Inside were two Mercedes Benz automobiles. The one on the left was a convertible with the passenger door open. Below it, on the garage floor, was a red towel and a woman's black high-heeled shoe. Officer Hockom looked into the car. The keys were in the ignition and turned to the first on position. The key chain read, "Richard's Keys."

Officer Hockom walked around to the front of the car, where he side-stepped a very large pool of liquid that had formed on the floor of the garage under the engine area. The hood was hot although the car was not running. The headlights were on and starting to fade. Apparently, the battery was dying.

He walked over to the other car and noticed the engine area was also hot. The keys were in the ignition, and the key chain read, "Janyce." He noted that a man's sport coat, tie, and belt were in the car.

He walked over to the door leading into the house from the garage and went in. The scene was chaotic. Inside were several police officers, as well as several first responders from the fire department. Everyone was asking questions trying to determine what was wrong with the victim. No one seemed to know whether or not the woman had attempted suicide or had a heart attack.

In the meantime, Officer Huffman took a quick look around for signs of a struggle. The house was well kept and tidy, except for what appeared to be dog feces on the dining room floor. A Rocky Mountain newspaper was lying on the breakfast room table, with a few pages scattered on the countertop. He walked through the rest of the house on the main floor and then went upstairs. The only thing out of place up there was a hairbrush lying on the floor of the master bedroom.

He returned downstairs and watched as the Fire Department personnel were working on the woman trying to revive her. One paramedic was giving her mouth-to-mouth resuscitation, while another was trying to get information as to the woman's age and anything else that would be helpful.

"Is this your wife?" he asked Richard. "How old is she? Do you know what happened to her?"

Richard didn't answer any of his questions. He was hysterical and acting as if he couldn't comprehend a word he was saying. The medic, desperate for information, turned his attention to Patricia.

"Do you know this woman? Is she your mother? Do you know how old she is? Can you tell me anything that might help us?"

Patricia just stood there crying uncontrollably and didn't speak either.

Officer Turner went in search of anything that would give them any information about who the woman was. Upstairs he found a purse on a bathroom vanity in the master bath. It was easy enough for him to retrieve a driver's license and identification. He went downstairs to convey the information to medics. The woman's name on the driver's license was Janyce Hansen, age forty.

After working on the woman for several minutes, it became apparent to the paramedics that they could not revive her. A medic then turned to Richard.

"I'm sorry, sir. She's not responding at all, and I'm afraid we can't do anything further for her."

They placed a sheet over her body and left. Then they notified the coroner and crime scene investigators.

* * *

Richard's parents lived only a few minutes away. They had already arrived and were waiting outside on the front driveway. After Richard was given the news about Janyce, he went out to be with them. Officer Huffman followed him out of the house and over to where he was standing. After verifying the identities of Adolph and Violet Hansen, he asked them when they last saw Janyce. They both said they had just seen her that day because they had spent most of the day in court with the couple.

Officer Huffman asked if they knew of any problems between Richard and his wife.

"No," Violet said. "They got along well, and they were both in good health."

Richard had somewhat settled down, so Officer Hockom took the opportunity to question him.

"Okay, Mr. Hansen. We need to sort out what happened here tonight. Take me back a few hours and lead me up to when you called for help."

Richard told his version of what happened. As he spoke, Officer Hockom noted that he seemed very intoxicated.

Richard's statement

"My wife and I had been out for the evening. When we returned home, I discovered that I had left my jacket at the restaurant. I told Janyce I was going to go get it, and I asked her to meet me at the Loading Dock restaurant for a drink. I went to the Loading Dock, and I waited for Janyce for about an hour. She never showed up, so I went home.

I pulled into the driveway and opened the garage door with the automatic opener. As I drove in, I noticed the Mercedes convertible parked in the garage had its headlights on, but the engine off. As I got out of the car, I saw my wife sitting in the driver's seat, and her upper body was slumped over onto the passenger seat. I also smelled a strong odor of carbon monoxide in the garage.

I opened the passenger door and pulled her out. She was unconscious, so I dragged her into the house and gave her artificial respiration. Then I called the fire department for help."

As he was telling his story, he became very hysterical again, so Officer Hockom was unable to speak with him further.

Then the officer went to question Patricia Hansen.

"Are you related to the victim?"

"Yes," Patricia said. "She's my stepmother."

"I want you to explain to me, to the best of your knowledge, what happened here tonight," the officer said.

Although still visibly shaken, Patricia was composed enough to tell her story. "When I arrived home at 8:00 p.m., Dad and my step-mom were both gone.

I went to sleep at 9:00 p.m. I woke up to hear my dad yelling on the phone to the fire department or police."

Officer Hockom asked, "Do you recall what time that was?"

"It was 2:55 a.m. Then I went downstairs and my dad was on the phone and my step-mom was lying on the floor."

"Did you hear any arguing going on before?"

"No," she said. "They both get along fairly well."

"That's all I have for you now," the officer told her. "Keep yourself available in case we have further questions."

* * *

CSI Agent McGoff arrived at 3:15 a.m., just as the Hansens were leaving. Richard and Patricia would be staying at Adolph and Violet's house while Agent McGoff processed the scene.

As he walked over to the open garage, Sergeant Davis met him and shared what Mr. Hansen and his daughter had told him about the night's events.

Agent McGoff took notes as to what he saw in the garage. He then went into the house from the garage. The victim lay on the floor covered with a white cloth. He lifted it and noted that her eyes were partially opened and glazed. The blue dress worn by the victim was cut down the front (due to resuscitation efforts). She wore only pantyhose under the dress, and she suffered no discoloration. There were no signs of bruising. The fingernail on the index finger of the victim's left hand was broken. She was wearing a gold ring on the left hand, but not on the ring finger.

* * *

The Arapahoe County Deputy Coroner Jeff Nielsen arrived at 4:00 a.m. Agent McGoff and Officer Hockom guided him through the scene, informing him there was no note left by the victim, and she was in good health. The only people there besides the victim were her husband and his daughter, Patricia. They did have a live-in maid, Nancy Jacobs*, but she was spending the night with a friend.

"The daughter did say something a little curious," Hockom told McGoff. "She was overheard saying to her father that she couldn't believe he was acting that way. Then she said, 'Dad, you suck.' She refused to ride in the same car with him when they left to go to his parents' house."

Agent McGoff processed the scene, taking twenty-one photographs, which included the victim, vehicles in the garage, a pair of woman's black high-heeled sandals, red towel, and women's purses upstairs on the bathroom vanities. He collected evidence taking a sample of the liquid that had pooled under the car, the red towel that was found on the garage floor, and the pair of woman's black high-heeled sandals. He would take the items back to headquarters, tag them, and enter them as evidence. Next he secured the residence and placed crime scene tape around the perimeter of the house and garage. In the meantime, the deputy coroner took possession of the corpse.

EIGHTEEN

The shrill sound of the phone ringing awoke Molly from a deep sleep. She nudged her husband as she was getting out of bed.

"Ben, wake up. The phone is ringing."

"What the hell time is it?"

"Almost four-thirty," she said, as the persistent ringing made her hurry to answer it.

"Molly?" The voice on the other end sounded anxious. "It's Violet Hansen. Something has happened at Richard and Janyce's house. You need to get over there immediately." Before she could respond, Violet had hung up.

Molly rushed back to tell Ben what Violet had said.

"Well," he replied, "if I have to go over there, I'll kill the son-of-a-bitch. He's probably drunk and beating on Janyce again. Everyone warned her not to go back to him."

"Just stay here," Molly told him. "I'll call Helen."

* * *

On the short drive to Richard and Janyce's house, Helen and her mother discussed different scenarios as to what may have happened to cause Violet to call so early in the morning. With all their speculation, they were in no way prepared for what they were about to find out. They couldn't possibly imagine what had transpired at Janyce's home just a few short hours ago.

It was about 5 a.m. when they arrived. As they drove closer to the house, they noticed several squad cars parked in the street.

Helen pointed at the house. "Mom, look. There's crime tape around the house. Oh my God, what happened?"

They pulled up in front and parked the car. The garage door was open, and two men in uniform were leaving it and walking over to their car. Molly and Helen got out of the car. They both had a sick feeling in the pit of their stomachs, much as if they felt a few months earlier when they learned Richard had beaten Janyce so badly that she ended up in the hospital.

After verifying who they were, Officer Hockom sympathetically informed them of Janyce's death, explaining that Mr. Hansen returned home to find her in the Mercedes convertible.

"The garage was filled with a strong smell of carbon monoxide, and she was unresponsive," he said. "Mr. Hansen took her into the house and attempted artificial resuscitation. He then called the fire department, and they were unable to resuscitate her."

With tears streaming down her face and her voice shaking, Helen said, "I just had lunch with my sister yesterday, and everything was fine." Her grief was turning to rage "My sister didn't die of her own free will. Last Thanksgiving, Janyce's husband beat her up so badly that she ended up in the hospital, and he was arrested by Denver police. I know Richard did this to her. He's a powerful man and was a mean, controlling husband. She did not purposely take her own life. You better check out Richard Hansen, because I know that son-of-a-bitch killed her."

All this time, Molly had been crying uncontrollably, and the other officer was trying to calm her down.

She kept repeating, "No, not our Janny. What happened? No, she can't be dead."

Helen realized her mother must be in a state of shock. She needed to get her away from there now. They would later regret not having arrived before the coroner took Janyce's body to the morgue.

* * *

It was Thursday evening, September 20, 1984. Jill had just finished packing for a weekend getaway. Nancy the maid had won a two-day trip to Vail, and she invited Jill to go along for a girls' weekend. Jill's boyfriend was out of town, so she agreed, and Nancy was spending the night at her house.

They ate pizza, listened to music, and talked with anticipation about the upcoming trip. Although it was supposed to be a ski trip, they didn't want to wait for the snow and planned to do some hiking on the trails and take in all the beauty of the changing fall colors and the aspens. They were also looking forward to doing some shopping and just hanging out at the resort.

Since they wouldn't be getting much sleep over the next couple of days, they turned in early. Jill was still sleeping when the phone rang at about 5:30 in the morning. It was Kathy, Richard's daughter.

"What's wrong?" Jill asked. "Why are you calling so early?"

"You need to get dressed and go over to Nanny and Poppy's house."

Jill protested, but Kathy was adamant. "Get dressed and get over here now," she repeated. Then she hung up.

Jill sensed the urgency in Kathy's voice and assumed something had happened to Nanny and Poppy.

In the meantime, Nancy woke up.

"Who's calling so early?" she asked. "What's going on, Jill?"

"I just got a weird phone call from Kathy. She wants me to go over to Richard's parents' house. I don't know why, but she said to hurry. I'll call you as soon as I find out what's going on. In the meantime, get ready to go. I'll be back as soon as I can."

* * *

There was no traffic, and Jill figured she could be at Nanny and Poppy's in about ten minutes. She hoped nothing bad had happened to them. They were good to her, and she did care about them. It was their son, Richard, she hated, Daddy Dicky. She tried to push the image of him out of her head, telling herself that jerk had ruined enough of her life. She was not going to let him ruin her weekend.

Jill glanced into her rearview mirror. She hadn't even washed her face, let alone put any makeup on. That was the least of her worries. Everyone told her she looked just like her mom, and she knew her mom was beautiful.

Soon she arrived at Nanny and Poppy's townhouse. As she walked up the sidewalk, she could see Richard through the window. He was sitting on the couch with his back to her.

She ran up to the door and rang the doorbell.

Niles, Richard's oldest son, came out and quickly shut the door behind him.

"What's going on?" Jill asked.

"Your mother is dead," he replied in a matter-fact-tone. "Now, go to your grandmother's house."

He turned and abruptly went back into the house, leaving Jill standing there alone. It was as if he had spoken the words in slow motion. *Why would he say that to me?* she wondered. There was certainly never any love lost between her and Niles, and it was no secret that he hated her mom. But to pretend her mom was dead was a little extreme, even for him. How could he be so cruel?

Jill turned around and started running toward her car. She tripped on the curb and fell, and then started crying.

Kathy and Patricia came out of the townhouse and ran over to her.

Looking up, Jill said "Niles just told me that my mom is dead. Is that true?"

"She did die," Kathy said. "I'm so sorry." She helped her to her feet and tried to console her. Jill was crying uncontrollably and in no condition to drive. Kathy offered to drive her over to her grandmother's house, and Patricia would follow in her own car.

On the drive, Jill asked what happened to her mother.

"I'm not sure," Kathy said. "Dad found her in the car in the garage. They think she might have committed suicide."

Jill couldn't believe what she was hearing. Her mother couldn't have committed suicide.

She rested her head against the back of the seat and thought about her mom. She wondered if Richard killed her, and if that's why his kids were saying that she committed suicide. There were plenty of times that she and Johnny told their mom to get away from him before he killed her. She would always reply, "He'll never let me go. I can't just get up and leave him. No matter where I go, he will always find me and drag me home. That is, if he doesn't kill me first."

Regardless of what Kathy wanted to believe, Jill knew there was only one way her mother could have died. And only one person responsible for her death.

NINETEEN

Shortly after 6:30 a.m., Kathy dropped Jill off at her grandparents' house. She walked in to see them and her Auntie Helen and Uncle Ted in the living room. Her grandparents were so grief-stricken they couldn't acknowledge anyone.

"You better not cry," Auntie Helen told her. "I don't want Grandma to hurt any more than she does already."

I'm hurting too, Jill thought. *My mother is dead. Why doesn't anyone ask me if I'm all right?*

While she walked around the room trying to comfort anyone she could, it seemed everyone had their own story of what happened to her mom. Jill just listened, because she still had not heard for sure how her mother died. There were so many different stories. Everyone seemed to believe Richard had killed her. Her grandparents were the strongest believers of that scenario. They always hated him and had predicted that someday something like this would happen.

* * *

Ben and Molly Bloom were born and raised in Denver. They planned to continue living there for the remainder of their lives. They had reared two successful, beautiful daughters, and their lives continued to prosper.

The Blooms acquired much of their wealth by working hard and investing in real estate. Ben purchased ownership in a tavern hot spot on Sheridan Boulevard called Hart's Corner from Ted, Helen's husband. Ben had also worked as a salesman for Coca Cola for many years. Before retiring, he worked as the purchasing agent for the Regency Hotel in Denver, which Ted and his family built, owned, and operated. Ben was in charge of ordering all the liquor for the hotel. Until her retirement, Molly worked as a bookbinder at a Denver printing company.

Janyce was eight years younger than Helen, and both of their daughters were married to successful real estate developers and investors. Richard and Ted practically built and developed half of the Denver metro area. They hired architect Roland Wilson to design many of their individual projects, including housing developments, apartment complexes, hotels, and restaurants. Together, they were worth millions as well as very powerful and successful businessmen individually.

* * *

Within hours of receiving the news of Janyce's death, Richard's side of the family, including his children, Niles, David, Linda, Kathy, and Patricia, were at his parents' home. Janyce's family, including her two daughters, Jaqueline and Jill, her sister Helen and her husband Ted, and their son Ron*, were at her parents' home. Helen's daughter, Brenda, was living in Phoenix and would be flying into Denver later that afternoon. Richard and Janyce's son, Johnny, who was serving in the U.S. Army, still had not been notified.

The families grieved separately, and with good reason. It was no secret that everyone present at the Bloom home hated Richard. He had always made them feel uncomfortable. Ben had a bad feeling about him from the first time they met. He never accepted Richard as his son-in-law or welcomed him into his home. Janyce's family often said just being in Richard's presence made them shudder. He seemed surrounded by an aura of pure evil, like the Grim Reaper wearing a suit. When he spoke, they said the hair on the back of their necks stood up. All the years their Janny was married to him, Ben's feelings of hatred toward Richard never wavered.

The first time Ted met him was when Janyce brought him to the Four Winds, an establishment Ted and his family owned. They arranged to meet for dinner. Janyce thought the two of them might be interested in investing in some apartment buildings together. Ted's first impression was that Richard looked like "the angel of death."

"Richard had an almost ashen appearance about him," Ted said, "and when I looked at him, I saw a skull and crossbones. When he spoke, it was as if he would not let the whole word come out, but would force it out through his teeth."

Janyce's family didn't think that she died of carbon monoxide poisoning, and they knew she would never have committed suicide. They believed that somehow Richard killed her, then put her in the car and set it up to appear as if she had committed suicide. They speculated that he may have strangled, suffocated, or drugged her. She could have fallen into a drugged or intoxicated sleep on her way home, and Richard left her in the car with it running and then took their other car to go to the bar under the pretense of finding his jacket.

The fact that he had not even tried to contact any of them only added to their suspicions. Helen and Janyce were very close and considered themselves best friends. Why wouldn't he at least try to phone his mother-in-law and offer his condolences?

Helen knew one thing was for sure. An autopsy would show what really happened. Hadn't she heard somewhere it was standard procedure to perform one when the cause of death was a suspected suicide or even undetermined? She wasn't going to wait and find out; she was going to call the coroner. Besides, she had a few other questions to ask, and she wanted to see her sister's body.

Thus she gathered her wits about her and made the call to the coroner's office. When she spoke with Assistant Deputy Coroner Ken Wilks, she let him know how she thought her beloved sister died and the person who killed her.

Mr. Wilks responded by telling Helen that Janyce was definitely alive when she was in the vehicle, as the level of carbon monoxide in her body was 80.4 percent, which is four times the fatal limit for carbon monoxide poisoning. Her alcohol level was also .197 and going up. He said that, other than alcohol and caffeine, there were no other drugs or substances found in Janyce's blood or urine. He also advised her that he found *no* marks, bruises, contusions, or signs of force, or violence on her sister's body.

At this point, Helen doubted what he was telling her and said she wanted to come down and view her sister's body.

"When someone dies of carbon monoxide poisoning, the victim's body becomes swollen and discolored," he said. Therefore, he advised against it, and she would not be able to view the body.

Helen had no choice other than to accept what he had said. She ended the call by telling him they would be eagerly waiting for the results of the autopsy.

TWENTY

Detective Victoria Lovato and Detective Dale Sims also assisted with the investigation into Janyce's death. The detectives were never called to the Hansens' home to be able to view firsthand what had happened. They only learned about the death when they reported to work the following morning, at which time they were assigned to the case—nearly five hours after officers were originally dispatched.

They began the investigation at the home of Adolph and Violet Hansen, Richard's parents, at 9:20 a.m. on September 21, 1984. Adolph and Violet greeted them at the door and told them that Richard had taken a walk to the park with his two sons, David and Niles.

Detective Lovato asked if they had been in contact with either Richard or Janyce recently. Violet said she and her husband had spent the last four days involved in a civil trial with their son. She went on to say the trial was initiated by Richard, her husband, and herself in reference to a breach of contract on a business deal. She and her husband were to manage an apartment building that Richard's company had built and that they had financed.

When they asked about Richard's state of mind during this period, Adolph said his son was very stressed over the whole ordeal. Violet added that the four-day trial had ended in their favor. However, they were not completely satisfied with the monetary decision.

Detective Sims asked if Richard or Janyce were known to drink to excess. Adolph answered that he and his wife often went out for lunch or dinner with them, and that neither drank during dinner. He said he wished he and his wife got along as well as Richard and Janyce did.

Both detectives questioned Patricia. After reiterating what she had told the officers previously at her home, she went on to say there were no disturbances at the house, and that nothing woke her from 9:00 p.m., when she went to sleep, until she awoke at 2:50 a.m. to hear her father on the telephone yelling to the police, "Janyce is dead." Patricia said she was sure she would have awakened if she had heard anything before that, as her bedroom adjoined the master bedroom, and her bedroom door was open.

The last time she saw her parents was when they left the office to go to dinner about 6:00 p.m. the evening before. She knew this, because she was self-employed as a nail artist, and her parents had an office right next door to her suite on East Hampden Avenue. Her dad and step-mom stopped by for a few minutes to say goodnight before they left for the day. They both seemed in good spirits. Patricia said it was quite normal for her parents to go straight from work to dinner. They did that almost every night.

Asked about her stepmother's fingernails, Patricia said Janyce had acrylic nails, and they often break very easily. Furthermore, if she broke one, she would not attempt to repair it herself.

Detective Lovato asked Patricia if she was aware of any problems her parents had with alcohol. She replied that neither of them had drunk alcohol for over a year. When the detective asked why they had stopped drinking. Patricia replied, "For no apparent reason."

Detective Lovato then asked Patricia about an incident in which her father allegedly assaulted her stepmother approximately one year before in November of 1983. She replied that her parents had been drinking during that incident. The detective asked if that was why her parents stopped drinking.

"I guess so," she said. She also admitted that in the past her parents had problems with drinking and violence, and she reiterated to the detectives that they had been getting along very well since they stopped drinking, and they didn't keep any alcohol beverages in their house.

Nor had her stepmother appeared depressed or unhappy about anything. However, Patricia further went on to state that work for her stepmother had been very stressful and frustrating lately.

When questioned about keys in the vehicles at the Hansen residence, Patricia told them that the keys were normally left in the cars in the garage.

In the middle of questioning, Violet went to answer the telephone. It was her grandson, David. He wanted Violet to tell the detectives that he and Niles were with their dad at the Aurora Police Department and wished to talk to them about this investigation. She relayed the information to the detectives.

As they were leaving, Violet remembered that no one had informed Johnny of his mother's death.

"Johnny is Richard and Janyce's son, and he's stationed in the Army at Ft. Stewart, Georgia," she said, "but that's the only information we have."

The detectives left saying they would take care of it.

Violet could not hold back her tears any longer. Poor Janny. She loved her daughter-in-law. Now her son wouldn't have his wife, her children wouldn't have their mother, and her grandchildren wouldn't have their grandmother. She imagined Johnny getting the news of his mother's death, and it made her sob harder. The last few hours had been like a nightmare. First, the hysterical phone call from Richard and Janny's house at 3:00 in the morning to say Janny was dead. Then going to their house, seeing all the emergency vehicles, all the policemen, then seeing Janny on the floor, dead. She had to wonder why Patricia would say, *You suck Dad* to Richard, then refuse to ride in the car with him. Why would Janyce kill herself?

She couldn't try to sort it out now. She knew she had to pull herself together for Richard's sake. However, she must have wondered why Richard didn't think to call his own son and let him know his mother was dead, especially knowing the bond that Janny had with Johnny.

* * *

Detectives Lovato and Sims returned to the Police Department. Richard was there waiting with his two sons, Niles and David, and his daughter Kathy. Detective Lovato escorted Richard to an adjoining room to question him, while Detective Sims stayed in the room to speak with his children.

David volunteered that he ran a company for his father, and business had gone well lately. A lot of positive things had happened for his dad and step-mom in the last week. Janyce had been working extremely long days for about three weeks to get the books together on a mobile home park they controlled that was having severe bookkeeping problems. It had just come together for her on the twentieth, and she was relieved. David also said that on the same day, the company he ran for his dad just closed the biggest deal it ever had. He believed his dad and step-mom had reason to celebrate on the previous evening.

Richard's kids were most likely there in support of their father, and not much more became of the interview.

In the next room, Detective Lovato listened as Richard gave his recollection of the previous night's events. According to the police report, he told the detective the following:

> "On Thursday evening, September 20, 1984, my wife of 24 years and I went to the El Torrito restaurant lounge. We arrived at approximately 6:30 p.m. We were both in good spirits at that time and, upon arriving, we went to the upstairs dining area and drank margaritas.
>
> We were having such a good time, we didn't bother to order dinner, and we continued to drink. We were just talking business. My wife was involved in setting up a new set of books for a trailer park we had just recently purchased.
>
> We were both drunk when we left. I don't know what time it was. I drove, and we were in Janyce's gold Mercedes 280SE heading home.
>
> On our way home, I pulled into the Loading Dock restaurant parking lot. I told my wife I wanted to go in and have another drink. She said no, she wanted to go home. So I continued through the parking lot and drove home.
>
> When we arrived home, I drove into the garage and discovered I left my

credit card at the El Torrito restaurant. I told my wife I wanted to go get my card and have another drink. She said she had a severe headache and didn't want to go with me. I told her to go in the house and have a few aspirins, and when she felt better, to meet me at the Loading Dock restaurant on Alameda. Janyce went into the house, and I left.

I drove to the Loading Dock, but I didn't go inside. I parked in a parking lot across the street from the restaurant and stayed in my car waiting for Janyce. I found my credit card on the floorboard—so I just sat in my car about forty-five minutes. My wife didn't show up, so I went home. I was away from home approximately one hour.

When I got home, I used the remote control to open the garage door. I drove in and parked next to my Mercedes, the 450 SL convertible. In time, I noticed the Mercedes' headlights were on, and the car was not running.

As I stated before, that's when I got out, found my wife lying on the front seat of the car, and pulled her out of the car and into the house. I noticed a strong odor of exhaust in the garage and in the house. I opened the front doors of the house and called for an ambulance."

Detective Lovato asked Richard if he had any ideas as to what happened.

"I don't know what could have happened," he replied. "My wife hasn't been depressed or unhappy about anything lately. We were getting along fine. We didn't argue prior to me going to the Loading Dock. However, as I told you before, I wanted to go out and have another drink, and she didn't want to."

Detective Lovato asked Richard about the assault on his wife about a year ago. Richard said that they had been happily married for twenty-four years. During the twenty-four years, there was only the one incident, that being the time when he assaulted his wife at the Denver Marriott Hotel SE in November 1983. He didn't want to go into the details of that incident.

* * *

On Friday, September 21, 1984, Detective Lovato contacted the coroner's office and spoke with Assistant Deputy Coroner Ken Wilks. The purpose of the phone call was to find out if the preliminary tests had been completed on the victim. Mr. Wilks informed Detective Lovato of the results, and said that Helen, the victim's sister, had recently called him and he had advised her of the test results.

Detectives Lovato and Sims continued their investigation by responding to the home of Janyce's parents. Neither was in any condition to answer questions, so the detectives spoke with Ted and Helen. When asked about Janyce's state of mind and overall health, Helen said her sister was in very good health with no problems, and she volunteered the name of Janyce's personal physician.

"I just had lunch with my sister yesterday," Helen said. "She told me things were going fine, and she wasn't unhappy or depressed about anything. Janyce told me everything was fine between her and Richard, but I really doubt it. Last November at The Denver Marriott Hotel SE, Richard beat her so severely that she had to go to the hospital. He was arrested by the Denver Police at that time, but Janyce did not pursue charges against him. That led to a separation between them. I know that my sister was afraid of him. Not only has he been violent to Janyce in the past, but also to her children."

Detectives noted that while speaking with Ted and Helen, they both reiterated several times they were suspicious regarding the circumstances surrounding Janyce's death.

As the detectives were getting ready to leave, Jill, the victim's daughter, stated that she had something she would like to tell them.

"I spoke with Patricia," she said. "She told me that Richard told her that he and Mom had a fight because he had wanted to go to the Loading Dock and have some more to drink, but Mom didn't want to.

So Richard left, and when he came back, he found Mom in the Mercedes that was parked in the garage. How would Patricia know that if she was sleeping?"

* * *

The detectives followed up on Richard's story by going to the El Torrito restaurant. They arrived at 1:30 p.m. and obtained a copy of the charge slip and guest check for the evening. The guest check indicated that Richard and Janyce had two margaritas on the rocks, one liter of margaritas, two more margaritas, two Mexican coffees, one Mexican coffee, two Spanish coffees, and two additional Spanish coffees.

The waiter told them that Mr. and Mrs. Hansen were regulars, and he verified that they left the restaurant between 10:30 and 10:45 the evening of September 20, 1984. He was accurate with the time, as he had just punched out of work at 10:30 p.m. and was standing outside when they left. He said that they appeared to be happy and having a good time.

The detectives then went to the Loading Dock restaurant and contacted the owner/manager. He said that he personally knew both Richard and Janyce, and that they and their family were regular customers. They would come in to eat dinner, and on occasion, would drink a glass of wine or have a cocktail with dinner. After speaking with the owner/manager, and several other restaurant employees, the detectives were satisfied, that Richard had not been to the Loading Dock restaurant the previous evening.

* * *

Lovato and Sims had arrived back at the station about 3:30 p.m. After some discussion and comparing notes, they decided to make a couple of phone calls before they called it a day. Detective Lovato placed a call to Richard. She asked him again about the previous night's events. He responded with much the same answers as he had before.

She also wanted to know if he recalled seeing the red towel on the garage floor. He said he hadn't, and that he didn't put the towel in the garage. It could have been there all the time, as the Mercedes occasionally overflowed, and a towel was kept there for the purpose of wiping up the overflow.

He said he'd like to have the Mercedes 450SL checked in reference to any defects or malfunctions, in regards to the fact that the car battery was now dead. Detective Lovato arranged to have the car towed to the police department impound.

Detective Lovato placed a call to the coroner's office at 4:00 p.m. and spoke with Assistant Deputy Coroner Ken Wilks. He said that the Arapahoe County Coroner, Dr. Wood, was out of town, and that he had the final decision on an autopsy in this case. If an autopsy were done, it would be on Saturday afternoon, September 22, 1984. Aurora Police Department Crime Scene Investigators would be notified at that time.

TWENTY-ONE

By late Friday afternoon on September 21, 1984, the Bloom family had still not heard from Richard, or for that matter, anyone else on his side of the family. In following with the Jewish tradition, Janyce's body was to be buried within twenty-four hours following her death, unless an autopsy was required—which Janyce's family had requested. Even if there was no autopsy, burial would not take place on Saturday, because it is considered Shabbat (the Sabbath) meaning a day of worship. Burial would take place on Sunday. Jewish law mandates a simple pine box. Embalming is forbidden. Janyce would be buried in a white burial shroud (tachrichim), which is purposely kept simple to avoid distinguishing between rich or poor.

While the family discussed the arrangements, a call was placed to Richard asking if he was going to pay for the funeral. He said he would, and that was the extent of the discussion. Ben and Molly were thankful he didn't want to have any say in the planning of it.

Because they were constantly in the public eye, the Blooms had the opportunity to meet many people. They became well-known and admired in metro Denver, as well as in the Jewish community. Therefore, it was not surprising how many people came to their home to pay their respects. Even their presence could not keep the family quiet. They still put voice to every scenario that came into their heads as to how they thought that Richard killed their beautiful Janny. They all believed Janyce's death was a direct result of something Richard did to her. Whether the family intended for their visitors to hear their accusations against Richard or not, it wasn't long before word got out. Janyce Hansen was dead, and her son-of-a-bitch husband had killed her.

* * *

Cindy, Janyce's friend and racquetball partner, had just gotten to work that Friday evening. The hostess told her that Janyce had called and left a number where she could be reached. Cindy went into her office to return her call, assuming Janyce needed to either change the time or cancel the racquetball game they had planned for Saturday. She hoped she didn't have to cancel. Both of them looked forward to their two- and three-times-a-week play dates.

A woman, whose voice wasn't familiar to her, answered the phone. She asked to speak with Janyce. Jill came to the phone and told her that she was the one who had called her, and that she had bad news. Her mom had died early this morning, Jill said.

Cindy was completely stunned. For a split second, she tried to rationalize in her head that Jill's mom wasn't Janyce. Maybe Jill had a different mom, or maybe this was not Janyce's daughter. Anything but what she was hearing. But Cindy knew Janyce had a daughter named Jill. It had to be true.

She sat motionless, unable to move or speak, while Jill went on to say that it was suicide, that her mother was found in the car and apparently died from carbon monoxide poisoning.

"I'm sorry," she said. "I know how fond my mom was of you and that she treasured your friendship."

Cindy cried for what seemed like hours while her mind was processing what she had just learned. When she was capable of thinking, her first thought was what had Richard done to her? She didn't believe for a second that Janyce would kill herself. She would never do that, not in a million years. She loved her kids, grandkids, family, and life too much to do that. Cindy knew in her heart that somehow Richard was responsible for Janyce's death. Janyce had told her on at least two separate occasions over the last several months that she wanted to divorce Richard, but she knew he wouldn't let her go. She herself had witnessed his anger toward Janyce many times. Janyce was terrified of displeasing Richard. She had to be mindful of everything she said and did, or he would get angry and possessive. And he was mean.

Allowing her to play racquetball was one of the few times he let her out of his sight. Even then, he would often come over and stand at the window and watch them play. Cindy let out a pathetic little giggle as she thought of how she and Janyce would sit under the window and talk so Richard couldn't see them. It was funny to think they actually got one over on him. Janyce didn't dare let him see them secretly talking. And during those talks, she would often cry and tell Cindy how afraid she was of him, but that she didn't know what to do.

Cindy had seen the black eyes Janyce had tried to cover with makeup, and she couldn't understand why Janyce would never admit to her that Richard abused her. She wished she could have found a way to help her friend, but unfortunately she didn't know what to do either. Now Janyce was gone, and the loss was breaking her heart. The death of her dear friend was terrible, and even worse was the feeling that Richard had something to do with it.

Janny was a freelance model in the 50s and 60s, and one of Denver's best. She regularly appeared in magazines, newspapers, and television commercials--and on a few occasions, Johnny and Jill would appear along with her.

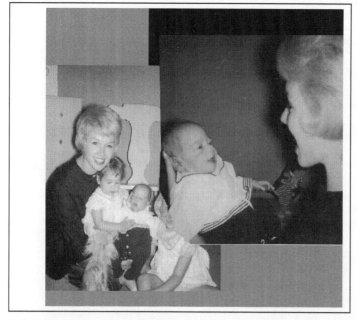

Janyce, a loving and doting mother, shown here with Jill (age 2) and her newborn baby boy, Johnny.

12G *THE DENVER POST Sunday, Nov. 1, 1970

Residence Complex Opened

Richard R. Hansen Enterprises has opened the first 16 of a planned 62-unit complex of Applewood Village Townhouses at 1788 Robb St. in Lakewood.

Ridgewood Realty, Inc., headed by Mike Leprino and ranked as Jefferson County's largest seller and developer of real estate, was named agent for the new condominiums.

The new complex contains two and three-bedroom units ranging in price from $27,000 to $28,500.

Along with full maintenance, Applewood Village offers private lanais, covered parking, underground utilities, swimming, park areas and a complete recreational building.

The units have more than 2,000 square feet of floor space each, with living, dining and kitchen areas on the main level, bedrooms and two baths on the second level.

"Happy Home owner" Richard

Town Houses 17th Robb October 1970

Opening of Applewood Village Townhouses, Lakewood, Colorado, October 1970--one of the first of many future residential projects by Richard R. Hansen Enterprises

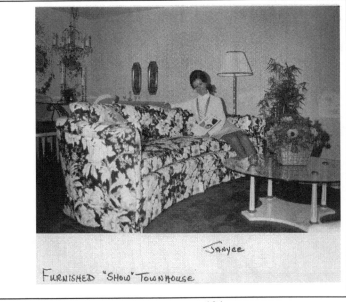

Janyce

Furnished "Show" Townhouse

Richard hired Janyce to model for his furnished "show" townhouses. Their affair began and they fell deeply in love.

Janyce at the construction site of The Cannery restaurant March 1972, off I25 and Yale in Denver, Colorado. Richard and Janyce envisioned the restaurant with a rustic exterior constructed of old barn wood and spent many weekends searching the Colorado Rocky Mountains and California for an old building. They found one in California, purchased it, then arranged to have the wood shipped back to Denver. Their plans were to turn The Cannery into a five-star restaurant serving the finest steak and lobster.

Richard, Janny, Jill and Johnny—Mexico was the Hansens favorite place to vacation. Richard would take the family two or three times a year. Photo on the left Juarez, Mexico April 9-12, 1971. Photo on the right Puerto Vallarta, Mexico August 13-21, 1971 (Jill 10, John 8)

102

Janyce with Johnny and Jill vacationing in the Colorado Rocky Mountains September 1971 (Jill 10, John 9)

Outside of the home, Richard made sure the family kept up their affluent and glamorous lifestyle. This family photo was taken for their membership into the Lakewood Country Club.

Richard, Janny, Jill and Johnny on a weekend ski-trip February 1973.
Richard was quite the family man and would include the kids
on their weekend getaways to Breckenridge, Colorado where they
owned a townhouse in "The Christiana".

Hansens' residence on E. Cedar Avenue, the dream home Richard and Janyce envisioned and built in 1980, and where Janyce died. They purchased the land and developed the subdivision with homes backing to the Aurora Hills Golf Course.

Richard and Janny were known for their over-the-top parties—tigers, belly dancers, DJ's, drugs, XXX movies, and orgies. These photos were taken at one of their parties on E. Cedar Avenue in August 1982.
The photo on the left shows Janny with one of the tigers.

Everyone always commented on how beautiful Janny was, and her daughter Jill looked so much like her. Shown on the left are Janny and Jill at Jaqueline's wedding.

Richard and Janny loved to play racquetball and were A players. They had a membership at the Denver Athletic Club where Janny met her best friend, Cindy Scott., shown here with her husband Buck.

106

In the early morning hours of September 21, 1984, Richard told the police he returned home to find his wife's lifeless body in the front seat of his Mercedes convertible parked in the garage, lights on, engine not running, and the strong smell of exhaust. He dragged her body into the house, attempted artificial resuscitation, and then called 911. Paramedics were unable to revive her. Janyce Hansen was dead at the age of 45.

A large puddle of unidentified liquid was in front of the Mercedes convertible. One of Janny's shoes was found in the garage and the other inside the house.

Photo on the left is the interior of Richard's Mercedes, the one he told police he found Janyce unconcious in. The keys were in the ignition and turned one click to the right, lights on, car not running. The key chain reads "RICHARD"
NOTE: The air conditioner is turned to the on position.

The photo on the right shows the interior of Janyce's Mercedes, the one Richard said he drove that night. The key is in the ignition and the key chain reads "JANYCE".

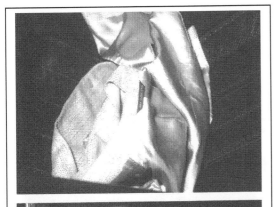

Richard's sports jacket, tie and belt were found in Janny's Mercedes--the one Richard said he drove that night.

The police found Janny's purse upstairs on the vanity in the master bathroom—no suicide note (top photo).
The bottom photo shows Patricia's purse in her bathroom.

John was away serving in the U.S. Army when his mother died. He was led to believe she committed suicide. Janny died just 5 days before his 22nd birthday.

John with his wife Kim. They currently live in Arizona with their two children, and will be celebrating their 23rd wedding anniversary November 2011.

Jill has never remarried. She lives in Denver near her children. Even though she has found a certain amount of peace through sharing her story, she continues to struggles with health issues and takes one day at a time. She has a close relationship with John and his family and visits them in Arizona at least twice a year.

TWENTY-TWO

Early Friday evening, September 21, 1984. The Red Cross had the information they needed to locate Richard and Janyce's son, Johnny. They in turn contacted the army base in Ft. Stewart, Georgia where Johnny was stationed.

When the army base received the call, they made all the necessary arrangements for him to fly home. Everything was set up ahead of time, so when he received the news of his mother's death, he would have just enough time to pack before the taxi would arrive and take him to the airport. Poppy, Richard's dad, would be the one to call.

Two-hundred twenty-five soldiers dressed in their khaki greens were lined up for the last formation of the day. The silence was suddenly broken when the Commanding Officer bellowed, "Specialist Hansen, front and center."

Johnny stepped out of formation. He was a lean young man standing six-foot-one-inch tall, with sandy brown hair and a winning smile.

As he made his way to the front, he wondered what could be so urgent that he was called out right before they were getting ready to fall-out. The Commanding Officer told him to report immediately to the Company Clerk's Office for a phone call.

As Johnny approached the office, the clerk stepped out of the room and closed the door after him. Johnny picked up the phone and answered, "Hello?"

It was Poppy, and he was crying.

"Johnny," he said, "I'm sorry, but I'm calling you with bad news. I hate to be the one to tell you this, but your mom is dead."

It took Johnny a few seconds to grasp what Poppy had said. When his mind finally accepted the words, his body went completely numb. Then a rage started in him like a scream trying to find its way out, working its way to a crescendo until he started going ballistic. He lifted the front of the desk up and pushed it over. The phone, papers, pens and folders went flying everywhere. He kicked the chair away from the desk as he reached out to the cabinets that lined the wall. Then he began yanking and pulling until they toppled over and crashed to the floor.

Hearing the ruckus, the Company Clerk and an officer came rushing into the room. They both grabbed Johnny and held his arms until he settled down, all the while trying to ease his rage with words of comfort. Johnny finally went limp and allowed the two men to help him to the barracks.

The taxi arrived shortly thereafter to take him to the airport. Johnny was on his way home.

* * *

As he boarded the plane, he was relieved to see that many of the seats were unoccupied. He was hoping that the one beside him would remain vacant as well. He wanted to sit alone, to be able to cry without some nosey person asking him questions like, "I couldn't help but notice you are crying. Are you all right? Is there anything I can do to help?" Then he would have to reply, "Hell no. There's not a damn thing you can do. My mom died this morning. She's dead. Now leave me alone." He would have to take his anger out on the nice person who was inquiring about his well being. Although the rage that took over his mind when he found out his mom was dead had subsided, he was still angry that she was taken from him.

The passengers finished boarding the plane, and the doors closed. The seat beside Johnny remained empty. Good. At least he would be able to grieve alone in the darkness of the plane. He could close his eyes and forget, at least for awhile, that he would never be able to see his beautiful mom again. He sat back in the seat, let his thoughts drift back to yesterday morning, and replayed their conversation in his head.

It was 8 a.m., and after finishing with PE, he had decided to call his mom. She answered on the first ring.

"Hi, Mom, it's me."

"Oh, hi, Johnny. I was just writing you a letter to send with your birthday card. Now, I guess I can just talk to you instead."

"No, Mom. You can still write to me. Please. I love getting your letters."

"I'm just kidding," she said. "Of course, I'll keep writing to you. I can't believe my baby boy is turning twenty-two in only six days. What are you doing today?"

"Nothing, Mom, just the regular stuff, like playing army. And speaking of army, I better make this quick."

"Okay. But please take good care of yourself, and try to call me again on your birthday."

"I will, Mom, and please send that card and letter off. I'll be looking forward to it."

"Okay. And please write me back. I love you, Johnny."

"I love you, Mom."

Johnny closed his eyes and allowed himself to cry, as he willed his mom back into his thoughts. This time, he thought back to four months ago. He had just finished eight weeks of boot camp in Fort Bliss, Texas. He flew home on a thirty-day leave and planned to stay at his parents' house on Cedar Avenue. His mom had come to pick him up. Her smile lit up the whole airport. They were so happy to see each other.

As they hugged, she said, "You look so handsome. I'm so proud of you, Johnny. You've grown up so much."

They'd always had a special bond. Often, they would be thinking the same thing, or both say the same thing at the same time. He was happy that she came alone to pick him up. At least he could have some time with her without his dad around to spoil things. She was like a different person when she wasn't around his father, carefree and happy. But then again, Johnny thought, they all felt different when he wasn't around. That was part of the reason he felt so close to his mom. She felt the fear, just as much as he and his sisters, Jaqueline and Jill, did.

Feeling that fear was pretty much constant. If someone asked you, using one word, to describe your feelings when you were growing up, what word would that be? Maybe you would reply by saying, happy or loved. Not Johnny. His word would be scared. He had always been on the lookout for his dad and was deathly afraid of him. If his dad decided Johnny needed a beating, he got one. His mom always left the room when he or his two sisters were getting, so-called, punished. She wouldn't help them, even if they begged her to. They knew the situation would only get worse for all of them if she tried to intervene, or maybe someone would even end up dead.

Often after one of his dad's drunken rages, his mom would come and find him, give him a big hug, and say, "Johnny, I'm sorry we're in this mess."

In his childish innocence, he would look up into her eyes and say, "Well, let's get out of it."

"We can't," she would reply. "Your dad will never allow us to leave. There is no place on this earth that we could hide from him."

When he was sixteen or seventeen years old, still in high school, he didn't have anything to do that morning and wanted to sleep in. His bedroom was in the finished basement of the house on Cedar Avenue. He heard his dad coming down the steps yelling something. The next thing Johnny knew, his dad was throwing a heavy glass ashtray at him. It hit him square on the mouth. He could feel the blood gushing out as he bled onto the sheets.

He stayed on his bed and yelled, "Oh my God. What did you do? What happened?" His dad left the room without doing or saying anything.

His mom came running down the steps, entered his bedroom, and seeing Johnny said, "Oh my God. What the hell did you do to him, Richard? Johnny, get up and get dressed. I have to take you to the hospital."

Then she helped him wash the blood off his face. She put padding on the cut and gave him some ice to hold on it as she drove them to the hospital. His dad had cut his lip wide open. Johnny received seven stitches.

When they got home, his dad didn't say a word about it. His mom knew better than to bring up the subject again.

* * *

The plane landing jarred Johnny awake. He must have dozed off. He wanted to go back to sleep until the pain subsided. But he was home back in Denver, and no amount of sleep could change what happened.

He exited the plane and walked up the ramp, wondering who would pick him up. He thought it might be his Poppy, since he was the one who called to tell him about his mom. He entered the airport with the other passengers. Some had loved ones who came to greet them, giving them hugs and kisses. Others just continued walking. He fit in with the latter group.

When he reached the baggage area, he didn't see anyone he recognized. He sat down to wait, put his elbows on his legs, and held his face in his hands. If no one showed up, he would figure out what to do next. He didn't know if anyone even knew he was coming home. He had no idea where he would stay during his thirty-day leave. He hadn't been living at home when he joined the army. He couldn't help but think if he hadn't gone away, maybe his mom would still be alive.

Before he joined the army, Johnny had been living with an old high school buddy, and dating Gloria*, a girl he met in high school. He referred to her as his Jewish Princess, the same name others called his mother, meaning neither one of them had to cook or clean. They always had hired help. They began dating in high school. After graduation, they continued their relationship through his college years, up until the time he enlisted in the army. After he graduated from high school, he attended Red Rocks Community College. His dad wanted him to become a geologist so he could help him with Diamond Hill Industries, Inc. Johnny was all for it, and in the fall of 1981, he enrolled in the Physical Geology and Petroleum Industry program at Red Rocks.

It wasn't long before his grade point average began dropping, and he decided to quit that college and enroll at the University of Northern Colorado, in Greeley. He was in a fraternity, Sigma Chi, and lived in the frat house.

He soon found out that old habits die hard. He continued drinking and smoking marijuana. Not only that, but he added gambling to his partying itinerary. Johnny's grade point average of 3.0 quickly plummeted, and he tried to justify his actions. What was a young college man to do? His parents basically paid for his downfall. They would send him blank checks. In turn, he would write them out for hundreds of dollars and cash them. His mom would question what he did with all the money. Of course, she always had a soft spot for her Johnny, so she believed him when he told her it went for books, tuition, and everyday necessities.

College life and party life; both took a toll on Johnny. He dropped out of college once again and begged his parents to let him move back in with them. They wouldn't allow it, because he wasn't attending school and didn't have a job. So, he turned to his old girlfriend, Gloria. She had an apartment. He moved in with her in the hopes of taking another shot at getting his act together. He decided to give college another try. This time he applied to Metro in downtown Denver and was accepted. Still he grew restless, and his partying continued. He moved out from Gloria's and in with an old high school buddy. Eventually, he dropped out of Metro. In all, he had attended almost two years of college. No degree. At this point, his father gave him an ultimatum. Either go back to college and get your degree or join the military. On March 8, 1984, Johnny chose to join the U.S. Army.

* * *

Someone tapped his shoulder. Johnny looked up to see his Auntie Helen. He stood to hug her, and they both started to cry. Johnny reached down for his duffle bag, and his Auntie Helen led him outside.

Neither said much on the short drive to Helen's. Johnny really wanted to ask her how his mom died, but he sensed she didn't want to talk about it.

It was after midnight when they arrived at Helen's. She and her husband Ted owned a beautiful home right off Monaco and Hampden in Denver. They had adopted two babies, Brenda and Ron, who were now grown and living on their own.

Earlier that day an official from Johnny's army base called the house of Richard's parents with information regarding Johnny's flight home. In turn, Violet called Helen and passed along the information. Helen was to make arrangements to have Johnny picked up at the airport. In anticipation of his arrival, Helen had a room prepared for his stay. After her conversation with Violet, it was obvious to Helen that Richard's side of the family didn't want Johnny at their home. You would think that Richard would want to have the only child around that he fathered with Janny, if for no other reason than to feel closer to her by being in his presence. This only served to add to Helen's suspicions about Richard being to blame for Janny's death.

Johnny thanked her for picking him up from the airport and then went to the room she had ready for him. He unpacked his duffle bag, hung up his dress greens and jacket, and placed his shiny black shoes on the closet floor. He'd wear these to his mom's funeral, along with his ribbons and hat. He wanted to show his mom the utmost respect.

* * *

The night was long and restless, and memories and dreams were relentless, as they seeped in and out of his head. He would doze off, jerk awake, and doze off again. One dream was so vivid that he almost believed his mom was really there. It was the time again when he just finished his eight weeks of boot camp and had been home on a thirty-day leave. When his leave was over, his mom had given him a ride back to the airport. They hugged each other tightly and said goodbye.

In his dream, he watched as she drove away in the Mercedes convertible. She was so beautiful. The sun lit up around her, as she turned and smiled at him.

She blew him a kiss and said, "You're finally out of this mess, Johnny." He felt the brush of her lips on his cheek as he woke up. He was certain she had been in the room with him. The light scent of her perfume still lingered in the air, and he could feel her presence.

Then he heard the sound of someone moving around in the kitchen area, probably making the morning coffee. It was 8:30 a.m., 6:30 a.m. in Georgia. He would have been up for a few hours by now. But he didn't want to get up yet. He wasn't ready to face the sadness and heartache that waited just beyond the door. He had enough in here, although he was kind of excited about seeing everyone. Of course, he would see his dad, Nanny, and Poppy, and his other brothers and sisters. He assumed that Jaqueline and Jill would be coming over, as well as his Grandma and Grandpa Bloom, and his two cousins, Brenda and Ron.

He really liked Ron. Despite their slight age difference, they were close and had gotten along well. In fact, he had some good times with Ron when their families got together. He remembered spending many weekends at his Auntie Helen and Uncle Ted's home in Dillon, Colorado. Uncle Ted had built a beautiful Swiss chalet house on the side of a mountain overlooking the soon-to-be Dillon Dam. The snow-capped Gore Mountain range was just behind it. Johnny, his mom, dad, Jaqueline, and Jill would spend weekends at their house. They would all go boating and hiking, just like a normal family. Johnny usually felt at ease around his dad if there were other people present. He didn't think his dad would start wailing on him in front of anyone else.

* * *

He must have fallen back to sleep. A knock on the door startled him.

"Johnny. It's Auntie Helen." Speaking through the closed door, she said, "Your Grandma and Grandpa will be here soon. I just wanted to let you know that they are both taking the death of your mother very hard, as are we. So please don't question them about it at all."

"Okay," he answered.

He could understand that. He was curious about how his mom died, but the fact that she was gone was upsetting enough. He could wait to find out the rest.

His grandparents arrived around mid-morning. Johnny did as he was told and didn't ask them any questions. But as the day wore on, he was sure starting to get a clear picture of how they thought she died. His grandma kept on repeating, "He killed our Janny. That bastard killed our Janny." Johnny knew she was referring to his father, and it was starting to anger him. Sure, his dad was an asshole, but for Grandma to outright accuse him of killing his mom just wasn't right. Maybe his sisters could fill him in on what was going on.

Jaqueline arrived around noon with her husband.

"Hi guys," Johnny said as he walked over to give Jaqueline a hug. They hung onto each other and cried. Then they looked at each other, both asking, "How long has it been since the last time we saw each other?"

Johnny thought it had been over two years, but he didn't know. It was hard enough just trying to remember what day it was now. Giving up, he put his hand on her shoulder and guided her towards the door leading into the backyard. "Come outside with me for a few minutes," he said. "I need to talk with you."

Once outside, they walked over to the patio area and sat down. Johnny lit a cigarette and took a deep drag. He was trying to compose himself before speaking. It was hard to talk about his mom without becoming emotional. After he exhaled, he asked Jaqueline, "How did Mom die?"

It took a few seconds before she replied. "I guess that she committed suicide."

"Who said that?"

"I don't know," Jaqueline said. "Auntie Helen, I think."

"Tell me what happened."

"The story I heard is it was around three in the morning, and your dad found Mom unconscious in the car in the garage. They had been out drinking. She must have left the car running and died from carbon monoxide poisoning."

Johnny pressed on with his questions. "Didn't anyone smell the carbon monoxide? Where were dad and Patricia? Wasn't there a maid? Where was she? Where was the dog? Why couldn't anyone help her?"

At this point, Jaqueline started to cry and said she didn't have any answers. Johnny was becoming upset. He pictured his mom sitting alone and dying, and no one coming to help her.

"Jaqueline, why does Grandma keep saying *He killed our Janny*? Is she talking about my dad? They don't think that my dad killed our mom, do they?"

"I'm sorry, Johnny. I don't know any more than you do about what's been going on. All I know is what I just told you. Remember, I've been out of the picture longer than you have, and Mom and I haven't been that close for the past several years."

They sat in silence for a few minutes. Then Johnny got up and told Jaqueline he wanted to find Jill so he could talk to her. He desperately needed answers. But after talking to Jill, he realized she didn't seem to know any more than Jaqueline did about how their mom died.

He was sure his dad would tell him everything. That is, if he could get in touch with him. No one answered at the house. When he tried calling Nanny and Poppy's, Nanny answered and told him that his dad was down in Colorado Springs. Johnny couldn't understand that. Why was his dad out of town? Shouldn't he be here helping with the funeral arrangements? He would wait until tomorrow. He was sure that his dad would call him to go to the funeral with him. Then he would give his dad as much love and support as he was able.

TWENTY-THREE

On many nights when Janyce went to bed, she took with her the memories of all the horrible things that had happened to her and her children. She would close her eyes and wait for her dreams to come and make all the terrible things disappear.

On several nights, she would lie awake for hours and cry, not only for herself, but for her children as well. But when she woke up the next morning, she was happy that another day had dawned, and with it, came another chance.

If Janyce were here, she would have loved waking up to this glorious, sunny autumn day. On this particular Sunday morning, upon rising out of bed, she would be looking forward to a long drive in the mountains with Richard. She loved the mountains, especially this time of year. The fall colors should be at their peak. She would grab a couple of glasses, a bottle of champagne, a blanket, and they would be on their way.

She and Richard would drive away in the Mercedes convertible with the top down. The warm sun would shine down on her face as the wind whipped through her hair. She would look over at Richard and visualize the man she had fallen in love with more than twenty-years ago.

As they wound their way through the mountain roads, Janyce would be in awe of the beauty around her. She would look at the blue sky reaching down to touch the tall pine trees that backed to the mountains. She'd watch a stream of water glistening in the sunlight as it trickled down the mountainside to a gully below. Golden aspens would blanket the slopes and valleys, their translucent leaves shimmering with the slightest breeze. They would drive until they got hungry. Then they would find a quiet little inn tucked into the mountainside where they would stop for lunch.

Upon entering, Richard would lead her to a small table in a secluded area of the restaurant. He would only have eyes for her as he held her hands from across the table and professed his love for her. They would share a bottle of wine while Richard told her all of the wonderful plans he had for their future together. After dining on seafood and hot buttered rolls, they would leave the restaurant arm in arm.

The mountain air was cool, so Richard would close the convertible top before continuing their journey. Their destination would be a place to watch the sunset. They would continue winding their way through the mountains, eventually pulling off the road and parking at the perfect spot. After putting their jackets on, they would get out of the car. She would spread the blanket on the ground while Richard poured the champagne. He would hand her a glass, then sit down beside her on the blanket. Then with his arm around her shoulders, he would hold her close, staving off the brisk Colorado mountain air.

As the sun was setting, they would look out over the magnificent splendor of the Rocky Mountains. They would hold onto one another and savor every last second of the beauty and love they felt for each other, as it reached into touch the very core of their beings. They would watch as the sun slowly disappeared behind the mountains. And as it disappeared, so did all of Janyce's hopes and dreams.

* * *

Her funeral would take place graveside at Rose Hill Cemetery in Denver. The families planned to meet at Helen and Ted's home on Sunday morning. From there, they would leave for the cemetery together. Ted, Helen, Ron, Molly and Ben left in one car. Johnny, Jill, Jaqueline and her husband, and Brenda followed in another.

The grieving family was among the first to arrive at the cemetery. They exited their cars and solemnly walked over to the gravesite where the services were to be held. Chairs were placed around the casket where Johnny sat down with Jill at his side, Jaqueline beside her, and the rest of their family facing the casket. Johnny sat motionless not wanting to believe that his beloved mother was in the wooden box in front of him. He wished his father would hurry up and get there. He needed his support to help get him through this.

The service was starting, and the chairs were still sitting empty. Johnny wondered why his dad hadn't arrived. His Poppy and Nanny weren't there either, and neither were his other brothers and sisters. He glanced around to see if maybe they were standing behind him somewhere and spotted Patricia, Kathy, and Linda. None of the others, though.

His mom's friend Cindy and her husband Buck had just arrived and were standing close to Ted and Helen. John searched through the sea of faces, but his dad was nowhere in sight.

The rabbi performing the funeral service was a family friend and had known Janny since she was a little girl. He had performed the ceremony at her first wedding. He spoke about what a genuinely warm and kind person she had been, and Johnny sat numb, wondering where his father was.

When the service was over, a hushed calmness came over the mourners. For a brief moment, everything and everyone was still, as if frozen in time. Then, suddenly, a gust of wind came and nearly took their breath away. At that instant, Jill looked up at a huge beautiful tree next to her mother's grave. The wind seemed to be blowing in that tree only as it swirled around the branches and leaves, and all the other trees remained motionless. Jill looked over at Johnny, with tears in her eyes, and he looked back at her with a knowing smile. Both felt a sense of peace, as if their mom was there with them.

The hand carved wooden casket was lowered into the ground. Each member of the family and the other mourners took turns shoveling dirt into the grave until it was covered.

As they left the cemetery, it was painfully obvious to the family that Richard hadn't been there. Others attending the funeral also questioned his whereabouts, whispering to each other as they walked to their cars.

* * *

Following in the Jewish tradition, it is customary for the family to sit Shiva (mourning) after the burial. Shiva would take place at Ted and

Helen's home. Many of the family friends and acquaintances stopped by, brought food and offered their condolences. Most of the visitors paying their respects knew Janny either as Helen's sister or Ben and Molly's daughter, not on a personal level.

Helen couldn't take it another minute. It bothered the hell out of her that Richard wasn't at the funeral. Just for a minute, she thought she would give him the benefit of the doubt. Maybe he was in jail. But she knew better. Detective Lovato would have called her immediately if that were the case.

She had been thinking about it since they left the cemetery, and it hurt her deeply to think that the man that Janny had stuck with all these years and loved unconditionally couldn't even show her enough respect to be at her funeral. She couldn't even wait for everyone to leave her house before finding out where he was. She was so angry she was going to call the son-of-a-bitch right that minute.

She sat down and placed a call to Richard.

He answered at once.

"Where in the hell were you?" she screamed into the phone. "Why weren't you at the funeral, you son-of-a-bitch?"

"What the hell do you care anyway? " he retorted. "None of you can stand the sight of me."

"For God's sake, Richard, she was your wife. Are you that callous? And not even to be there for your kids? You make me sick, you bastard. Why weren't Adolph and Violet there and your other two sons? What's their excuse?"

"We just couldn't take all that sadness," he replied.

"You know why you can't? Because you killed her," she said. "And when the police prove it, you'll end up rotting in some prison where you belong."

"I didn't kill your sister, you crazy bitch," he shouted into the phone. "Now leave me alone."

The sound of the phone being slammed down echoed in Helen's head.

Johnny had entered the room and overheard his Auntie Helen accusing his dad of killing his mom. He had just walked from the other room where he heard his Grandma Bloom telling his Grandpa Bloom that he killed their Janny.

"Our daughter is dead, and he killed her," Grandma Bloom was saying.

Johnny thought, sure, emotions were running high, and everyone was on edge. But he couldn't take this shit. He was getting the hell out of there. He used the phone to call David to pick him up.

About fifteen minutes later, David pulled up to the curb in his car and Johnny got in the passenger seat. After making small talk, he said "I had to get the hell out of there. Everyone is saying that dad killed my mom. All I've heard them talk about for the last two days is how Richard killed their Janny."

"That's bullshit, man," David replied. "The only reason they are saying that is because they hate Dad, and you know it. Your mom killed herself."

"That's bogus. Why would my mom kill herself?"

"I don't know," David said, "but I sure as hell know that Dad didn't."

"Why wasn't he at the funeral then, or you guys either? The only ones who came were Patricia, Kathy, and Linda."

"Dad didn't go because he heard they think he killed her. He didn't want us to go because it would make him look bad, but the girls went anyway. He's at Poppy and Nanny's. Let's drive over there now."

* * *

Not long after Johnny had left, Kathy and Patricia decided to stop by Helen and Ted's to see Jill. She thought that maybe Richard put them up to it after the nasty phone conversation their dad just had with her Auntie Helen. He probably wanted some inside information on what else was being said about him. Still, Jill had nothing against them. Not only were they her adopted sisters, they were also her friends.

As they talked, she started getting an ill feeling in the pit of her stomach. She noticed Patricia was wearing one of Janny's favorite blocked sweater dresses and a pair of her two hundred dollar black high-heeled shoes. Knowing her mom had recently bought the shoes on a shopping trip to the mall with her, Jill asked if Patricia had been at the house since her mom died. She told Jill that she and her dad didn't go home until Saturday. They would have Friday night, but for some reason, her dad had been too afraid to. So they stayed at Poppy and Nanny's. Kathy said she hadn't been there, yet.

Jill told them that Jaqueline, Brenda, and she had gone over there late Friday afternoon.

"When we went in, the first thing we noticed was the strong smell of exhaust," she said. "You could still smell it everywhere. We went into Mom's bedroom and looked around, and then went downstairs to look in the garage. It was like we could picture everything that happened, really creepy. We got scared and left."

She didn't tell them that they were terrified that Richard would come home and find them there—and that was the reason they left.

Jill was like her mother in many ways. Sometimes she was nice to a fault and never wanted to hurt anyone's feelings. She somehow felt everyone had a right to know everything. And she felt compelled to tell them certain things that maybe she shouldn't be sharing. On this day, she told Patricia and Kathy about one of the last conversations that she had with her mom. It was on the day before she died.

"Mom told me that she had a safety deposit box that no one else knew about," she began. "She said she had some things in it for me, Jaqueline, and Johnny, and she wanted me to be able to sign for it, in case anything ever happened to her. She wanted me to go to the bank with her, right then and there, so they had my signature on file, but I told her I couldn't. I had nail appointments all day. So I would have to do it some other time."

Jill barely got the words out of her mouth when Kathy asked if she could use the phone. *Why did I open my big mouth?* She thought. *The girls are going to call Richard and tell him about the safety deposit box.* That is exactly what happened.

What she didn't tell them was that she had seen safety deposit box keys on her mom's dresser the day she had gone there with Jaqueline and Brenda. She only wished she had taken them because she knew she wouldn't be allowed in the house again if Richard had anything to say about it.

After the phone call to their dad, Patricia and Kathy left. Jill sat down and wondered what possessed her to tell them about the safety deposit box anyway. She had wanted to tell them about the keys that she had seen on her mom's dresser the day that she, Jaqueline, and Brenda went over there. Now she wished she had taken them. But at the time she figured they weren't to the box her mom had wanted them to have, anyway. But then again, they were to something of her mom's.

She had only noticed them when she was looking through her mom's jewelry, only all that remained of it was just a bunch of wild looking, plastic baubles. Costume jewelry. She knew that low-life

Richard must have already taken her mom's nice pieces and hid it somewhere so he could give it to his other kids. She didn't tell any of that to Patricia and Kathy, though. Sometimes she wished she had the nerve to tell them what she really thought of their dad and what he had done to her. He had stolen her innocence and ruined her life, and she still could not speak up.

* * *

When David and Johnny arrived at Poppy and Nanny's house, Nanny welcomed Johnny with a big hug and guided him into the kitchen. She was one hundred percent Italian and believed the way to a man's heart was through his stomach. That's one of the reasons Johnny always liked going to his Nanny's house. Unlike his mom, who rarely cooked, Nanny was always in the kitchen.

Johnny sat down at the table. Nanny placed a glass of milk in front of him and David and offered them brownies. As Johnny ate them, he thought back to all the times he had come here with his mom and dad and sisters.

Both his mom and dad's side of the family were big on get-togethers. Whenever there was a holiday, or someone's birthday rolled around, there was a celebration. Sometimes as many as fifty people filled the house. All the Hansens and Frazzinis, from his Nanny's side, and everyone else brought their kids. Even his dad's ex-wife was there, with the five kids, celebrating along with everyone else. His Grandma and Grandpa Bloom were also included. A lot of them spoke Italian, but that didn't stop them from joining in the fun. They would set up tables, end-to-end, either outside or in the house, depending on the weather. When they were finished setting out the food, he couldn't see the table anymore.

Just then, he heard his dad come in the front door.

As they hugged each other, his dad said, his voice wavering, "Johnny, those bitches think that I killed your mom."

He pulled away and, with tears in his eyes, he asked, "What happened to my mom? How did she die?" Before giving him a chance to respond, he continued, "I've been away for months, and then I come home to this. What's been going on? Everyone is accusing you of killing her. That's all I've had to listen to for the last two days at Auntie Helen's, that Richard killed their Janny. It's starting to drive me nuts.

Why are they saying that?" His voice was growing louder, and the tears were coming faster.

"I'm sorry, Johnny. I don't know what happened," he said. "All I know is that we were on our way home after having a few drinks, and I realized that I left my jacket at the restaurant. I dropped her off at home and went back to get it. When I got home, I found her in the car. She died of carbon monoxide poisoning. That's all I know about it."

Johnny sat back down at the table and knew that he had lost the battle. His dad hadn't told him anything that he hadn't already heard. He put his head on his arms as they rested on the table, emotionally exhausted. The last two days had been more than he could handle.

His dad put his hand on his shoulder. "Come on, Johnny. Let's go home. You can stay with me until you have to go back to Fort Stewart."

TWENTY-FOUR

Cindy wanted to talk to Helen alone, so she waited for Shiva to end before going to see her. It had been over a week since she had received the news about Janyce, and she needed to find out the details surrounding her death. It was hard enough to accept someone dying naturally. How could Cindy accept the fact that her friend took her own life? She knew Janyce would never do that. Even when she seemed at her lowest, she accepted her life as it was. She would smile at Cindy through tears and tell her, "Everything will be better tomorrow." She was always concerned about everyone else's feelings.

Helen and Ted were both at home when Cindy and Buck arrived. Ted and Buck went into the den, while Cindy and Helen sat at the kitchen table. Cindy wasn't at all surprised to find out that Helen and Ted shared the same feelings as she did about Richard. They all hated him and were aware of how scared Janyce was of him.

"I know it's really painful to talk about," Cindy told Helen, "but I need to know how she died. Jill told me that Janyce was found in the car, and she died of carbon monoxide poisoning. My first reaction, when Jill told me, was that Richard killed her."

"That's exactly what we think too," Helen said. "Most of what we know about what happened that night is what he told the police. We don't believe his story for a second."

"Well, one thing for sure is not likely, and that is that Richard left Janyce alone at home," Cindy said. "He damned near had her on a leash and always made her go with him. I know he wouldn't leave her at home while he went to a bar. No way."

Helen said that she suspected Richard got Janyce drunk, and that she passed out in the car on their way home. Richard pulled into the garage and left her in the car with the motor still running, then got into the other car and left. When he returned home, he put the rest of his plan in motion.

Cindy was stunned. "Oh my God, Helen," she said. "Have you told the police about your suspicions?"

"Yes. Ted and I have made them very much aware of what we think happened. We also filled them in on some past issues that Janyce had with Richard, and how terribly afraid she was of him. We not only told the police, but we also told the detective who is conducting the investigation."

"Are they finding out anything? Do the investigators still think that it was a suicide?"

"They've only told us that the investigation is still ongoing, and they don't have anything new to tell us," Helen replied.

Helen also told Cindy that although Richard had agreed to pay for the funeral, he hadn't done so.

She explained that she had received a vulgar, hateful, letter from Richard that read: "I'm not going to pay a f***ing dime for Janyce's funeral because she wasn't buried the way I wanted her to be, head first with her legs spread apart."

Helen began crying. "I copied the letter and sent it to the detective," she said.

"How can any human be so cold blooded and heartless?" Cindy said. "I feel so bad for her kids. What do they think about how she died? Do they share in your belief that Richard killed their mother?"

"I honestly do not know what they believe about her death," she told Cindy. "I do know that both Jaqueline and Jill hate Richard. They have for years. As far as what John thinks, I don't know. I believe he's staying at the house with his dad until he goes back to the service. Ted and I hired an attorney for Janyce's kids after we found out about the safety deposit box. I just hope the attorney can put a freeze on anything he finds. That is, unless Richard has already had a hand in it. He has a way of turning things around to work to his advantage."

TWENTY-FIVE

A few days later, Helen received another letter from Richard. This one she hand-delivered to Detective Lovato because she wanted to see if there were any further developments with the case. When she arrived, Detective Lovato told her that Richard wanted to clear up any doubt that anyone had about his innocence. He volunteered to take a polygraph test in an attempt to clear himself. Helen handed the letter to Detective Lovato and told her that she was already aware of that, because Richard said so in a letter to her.

The following is the letter on file with the Aurora Police Department written by Richard Hansen and addressed to Helen. The letter has not been edited.

> *You and your family's accusations have embarrassed me and added to my mental anguish. I have requested to take a polygraph test from the Aurora Police just for your benefits.*
>
> *I expect you to advise every Jew in Denver of the results of my test. You have 30 days to do so and provide me with evidence of your efforts.*
>
> *If you do not make every effort to present the facts to everyone you have made accusations to, I shall file a lawsuit and pursue it until your entire family is bankrupt.*
>
> *My morals and business conduct have established a highly respected reputation for myself over a 30 year*

period. No one can or has ever accused me of any wrongdoing. I have never abused anyone or anything. Janyce was nearly perfect. She only crossed the forbidden line once in 24 years and we both suffered through the incident. I know his name and phone number.

Three times in the past two years, I have brought Janyce home and went out and continued partying. Each time when I returned home, she was gone. The first time she spent the night with Patricia, the second time she spent the night with Kathy and the last time she spent the night with Jaqueline. It was her way of punishing me for going out without her. Four times in 24 years should be acceptable. No one in the world has ever seen me out alone or with another girl at anytime.

The night she died, she was either coming to meet me or going to one of the girls again. I think she started the car to warm it up with the heater and simply fell asleep. It was a tragic accident.

Your loss is infinitesimal in comparison to mine. Your love and association was blood. My love and association was by choice and it grew stronger every year.

You must retract your accusations against me. They are unfounded and untrue.

Janyce told me a million times that I wasn't the best husband in the world but that there were none better. Do not continue to defile our marriage. I will not permit it.

Richard

Detective Lovato told Helen she would let her know the results of the polygraph when she received them. After Helen left, the detective placed a call to Richard and set up another interview with him before he took the test. Later in the day, he called back and said he didn't want to be interviewed again; he just wanted to take the polygraph.

After speaking with him, she contacted the Arapahoe County Coroner's office. A few days prior, she had spoken with Assistant Deputy Coroner Ken Wilks, and he had informed her that no autopsy was performed on Janyce, as Dr. Wood was unavailable, and the immediate family did not request one. When calling this time, she was able to speak with Dr. Wood, the coroner. Detective Lovato asked him if a subject exposed to carbon monoxide had passed out or was sleeping at the time they ingested the carbon monoxide, would the victim's eyes remain closed. Dr. Wood replied that it wouldn't make a difference. Usually the victim's eyes were closed, but they also could be open.

He went on to say that the victim is more susceptible to carbon monoxide when alcohol is induced into the body. As a result of the ingestion of the carbon monoxide, the victim does lose consciousness just prior to death, and the victim will sometimes get sick and vomit on occasion.

Later in the day, Detective Lovato received a telephone call from Richard. He said "I previously set up an interview for Monday morning. After thinking about it I have come to the decision that I will not be reinterviewed by you for two hours plus take the polygraph. I will do one or the other. I would prefer to take the polygraph so I can clear myself and put an end to this investigation. I am tired of talking about it."

"I will set up the test," Detective Lovato replied.

On October 1, 1984, Richard appeared for his polygraph test as scheduled. Before the test was administered, Richard signed a statement assuring everyone concerned that he was taking the test voluntarily. He also wanted the examiner to know that he was the one requesting the test.

Before beginning, Mr. O'Brien, the polygraph examiner, conducted a pre-test interview. Richard said that because he was so intoxicated on the night in question, he had no idea of the actual time-frame of the events on the evening his wife died. He also said that after leaving the restaurant, he and his wife had a disagreement over drinking, and that they did not talk on their way home.

The questions to be asked by the examiner were reviewed with Richard before the actual test. Here are three relevant ones along with Richard's responses.

(31) Did you intentionally cause your wife's death?
Answer: No
(33) Did you personally take any action
that resulted in your wife's death?
Answer: No
(35) Before leaving your home, did you

know you would find your wife in the car when
you returned?
Answer: No

Part way through the administration of the polygraph test, the police department, along with the rest of the northeast section of the city, suffered a power outage. Thus, the scores on this polygraph were not counted. Richard agreed to return on that Friday to submit to another test.

* * *

Prior to taking the second test, Richard said, "Before we start, I want to tell you that I have told big lies in connection with civil cases that I have previously been involved in. I also want you to know that in the past any time it served me, and if it would put me in a better light, I would lie to any authority."

The three questions were asked again. Then the following three relevant questions were each asked three times each:

(41) Other that what you told me, did
you knowingly lie to the police about the
circumstances of your wife's death?
Answer: No
(42) Have you lied about any action you
took that caused your wife's death?
Answer: No
(43) On the morning of September 21,
before you arrived home, did you know you
would find your wife in the car?
Answer: No

The tests showed that Richard's answers were deceptive on all relevant questions. Detective Lovato asked him to come down to the Aurora Police Department Headquarters to discuss the results.

When he arrived, she told him that his polygraph answers were deceptive.

"I felt guilty," he said, "and that's probably why. I feel guilty, because if I hadn't left that night, my wife would still be alive. I also lied when I told you that I asked my wife to meet me at the Loading

Dock. I told you that I went to pick up my credit card or my jacket. I didn't. After I dropped my wife off at home, I went straight to a private club in Denver. I didn't tell her to meet me anywhere."

"What's the name of the club?" Detective Lovato asked.

"It's none of your business," he replied. "I'm not going to tell you the name of the club or its location or what I was doing there. I can tell you that I didn't have any more to drink that evening, and I was not with another woman."

When Detective Lovato ended the interview, Richard said that he wanted to take another polygraph test.

Thus, he had yet one more test with Mr. MacDonald, a different examiner. This time, Richard said that when he found his wife in the car, her eyes were partly opened, and that he dragged her out of the garage, onto the driveway, and administered mouth-to-mouth resuscitation. When he realized the resuscitation was not working, he carried her into the house, laid her on the floor, and called the police. After going over the interview and pre-test with Richard, the following relevant questions were asked.

(1) During that Thursday night, did you do anything other than leave that contributed to the death of Janyce?

Answer: (No)

(2) Other than leaving her alone, did you cause the death of Janyce?

Answer: (No)

(3) Have you now told the entire truth about your actions on that Thursday night?

Answer: (Yes)

The above test was administered twice. The second examination follows:

(1) When you left Janyce home that Thursday night, was she in the Mercedes Convertible in the garage?

Answer: (No)

(2) Did you expect to find Janyce dead when you arrived home from the club?

Answer: (No)

(3) Did you kill Janyce?

Answer: (No)

The above questions were each asked three times. After a careful analysis of the charts, Richard indicated deception when answering all of the relevant questions.

Again, Detective Lovato phoned him with the test results. Richard didn't sound surprised or upset.

"I can't imagine what could be wrong," he told her. "I should have got 100 percent because I told the truth."

She asked him to come down to the Aurora Police Department Headquarters for an additional interview.

When he met with her and Crimes Against Persons Sergeant Jim Farrell, Richard admitted that he was still withholding some details. He said after he discovered his wife in the garage, and after the police responded and did the initial reports, he was sitting in a chair in his parents' living room. All of a sudden, he recalled his wife saying, "I'll wait for you in the garage."

He also said that when he went back to his house after the initial investigation, he found a notepad on a vanity, next to his wife's purse, in the upstairs bathroom. Then he looked through the wastebasket underneath the vanity and found a crumpled piece of paper that appeared to come off of the same pad. At the top of the paper, was the letter I and then H, and either an E or A. He felt that she wrote the note in conjunction with her telling him, "I'll wait for you in the car." He said he didn't volunteer this information before, because he was trying to avoid the stigma of a suicide.

The reason he made up the story about leaving his credit card at the restaurant was because he didn't want to say where he had really gone that night, he told the officers.

On October 12, 1984, Mr. MacDonald administered Richard yet another polygraph examination. During the pre-test interview, Richard told the examiner that previously he had not been completely truthful concerning his actions on the night that his wife died. He said the name of the private club he had gone to after leaving his wife at home was the Empire Baths.

He also repeated what he told the officers about the notepad and his suspicion that his wife had committed suicide, but this time he changed his story stating he found two of his wife's purses on the vanity, and the notepad with writing on it hanging over the counter a little way, as if placed to attract his attention. Then he tore off the paper with the writing on it and flushed it down the toilet. He was given two separate polygraph tests that morning, the first test having the following relevant questions.

(1) After you took Janyce home that Thursday night from the El Torrito, was she in the convertible when you left for the club?

Answer: (No)

(2) Did you expect to find Janyce dead when you arrived home from the club?

Answer: (No)

(3) Other than those times you went to the club, did you do anything to cause Janyce's death?

Answer: (No)

The second test was administered with the following relevant questions.

(1) Have you now told Detective Lovato the entire truth concerning this investigation?

Answer: (Yes)

(2) Were you truthful when you told me about that notepad you found the following day?

Answer: (Yes)

(3) Are you now withholding any information concerning this investigation?

Answer: (No)"

After careful examination, the examiner's opinion is that Richard indicated deception when answering all of the relevant questions. Question number (1) of the second test, concerning if he told detective Lovato the entire truth, was where deception was the strongest.

At the end of testing, Richard told the examiner, "I'll be willing to do more tests, and I'm willing to submit to further interviews. But I prefer not to be interviewed by Detective Lovato because of my association with Empire Baths, which is a homosexual club. It would cause me great embarrassment. I'm not gay myself. I just went there to visit the men."

Nevertheless, the examiner referred Richard to Detective Lovato for the test results. His response this time was that he never lied. He just withheld information. The only thing he withheld was the fact that he went to the private club, and he had done that out of embarrassment.

The thought of his wife committing suicide disgusted him so much that he tore up all of her pictures, he said. But he was still uncertain and thought it might have been an accident. Further, he was bothered by the fact that The Rocky Mountain Newspaper was found in the car, along with his wife's glasses. It was on the kitchen table Thursday morning before they left for the office.

Richard said that he and his wife usually had gone out two or three times a week throughout their marriage and were well-known at the discos and bars throughout the Denver area. Until recently, they would drink until the bars closed, but then his wife tried to change his lifestyle by going home earlier, and he didn't like that.

They usually got along pretty well, except on occasion when his wife would drink too much, and her personality would change, he said. Then she would become somewhat abusive towards him.

The polygraphs were over. Richard had insisted he knew nothing more, and on October 12, 1984 Detective Lovato closed the case. She reported that there was no evidence to indicate any signs of foul play in regards to Janyce's death. Nor was there sufficient information to either classify the case as suicidal or accidental. The case was closed with just as many unanswered questions and as much confusion as there was in the early morning hours when Janyce was found dead.

Many people wondered why it was closed when so much doubt remained. Didn't Richard flunk three polygraph tests? Didn't he admit that he would lie to any authority figure? He said he'd fought with Janyce on their way home that night and admitted that he was unhappy about her trying to change his lifestyle. Not only didn't he go to her funeral, but he poured salt on the wound by writing the nasty letter to Janyce's sister, Helen, and sent copies to Janyce's two daughters and her parents.

No one else but Richard mentioned anything about a suicide note, and it didn't show up in the crime scene photos. According to the investigators, there was no suicide note.

Why didn't the detectives confirm Richard's statement that they drove Janyce's Mercedes that day and not the convertible? The waiters saw Richard and Janyce drive away from the restaurant that night. Why didn't they ask the waiters what car they were driving? Patricia and Jill told family members and others that they saw Richard and Janyce driving the Mercedes convertible to work that day.

Why didn't they question the maid? What about Patricia? She was right there in the house. One would have to wonder why she didn't hear her dad yelling, but the neighbor did. Furthermore, why did she say to her father, "Dad, you suck," and refuse to ride in the same car with him when they left the house? Who did Patricia ride with? Who did Richard ride with? At the time, it was believed that Richard's only relatives there that night were Patricia and his parents.

Patricia told Jill that her dad said that he and Janyce had a fight about going back out that night. Why did he tell her that? Or did she witness a fight between them?

So the question remained. Did Richard cause his wife's death? Had he diabolically been planning to kill her? If so, what was the motive? Was he so set on carrying on his lifestyle of carousing that he would rather kill his wife than change?

These questions and many more would be brought up again, but not for another twenty-five years. It would take that long before a brother and sister would sit down together and talk about the past. Memories that were all but forgotten and buried away for many years would resurface once again. Maybe then they would be able to find the answers that they so desperately sought.

TWENTY-SIX

The rest of Johnny's thirty-day leave was spent in a fog. He spent most of the time staying in his old room in the basement getting drunk and had no idea where his dad was half the time. His dad didn't care anyway. He was off doing his own thing—partying, drinking, and doing drugs.

Johnny didn't know what to make of his behavior. He didn't talk about, or even seem to grieve for, his mom, whatsoever. Yes, he was in a bad mood for the most part, but he acted the way he would at some minor disruption like a flat tire.

Johnny only had a few days left before he had to go back to the army and spent the time sobering up. He was actually looking forward to returning. At this point, he needed direction, some type of normalcy in his everyday life. He wondered what it would be like the next time he came home. He did know that nothing would ever be the same again. His mom was the person who connected his life to everyone and everything, and now she was gone. How could he ever make that connection without her?

A few days later, Johnny returned to Fort Stewart. And all the questions he had about his mom's death went with him.

* * *

Jill was also having a hard time accepting her mom's death. Her boyfriend wasn't giving her much support, and she didn't want to intrude on her sister. Jaqueline was busy with her husband and baby. Jill knew that Richard must have had a hand in her mom's death.

She hadn't seen or talked to Johnny since the funeral. At least he had a place where he could stay and he could always call home—unlike her. She wouldn't be allowed in her mother's home ever again, not that she'd want to. The point was, she didn't have the option. Richard would make sure of that.

A couple of years ago when she was living in Arizona, Richard called her with a business proposal. He said he wanted her to move home and open a nail salon along with his daughters, Patricia and Linda. He offered to help her out financially, as well as finance her schooling until she became board-certified. Then he would set them up with their own business—and in no time at all they would be making tons of cash. It seemed Richard had a sixth sense when it came to starting a business and knowing where the money was. He was right on the cusp when the nail salon business exploded in the eighties.

True to his word, in no time, they were making tons of money. Besides the pay, Jill had some very generous tippers. They named the salon, The Nail Affaire, and they catered to a wealthy clientele. Jill kept them coming back. To her, doing nails was an art, and she was proud of her accomplishments.

Following Janyce's death, she decided to go back to work because she needed the money, and she felt it would help her emotionally if she could keep herself busy. When she arrived at The Nail Affaire, she tried to unlock the door and discovered her key didn't work. After a few more tries, she gave up. It was almost 9:30 a.m. She knew that Patricia would be coming to work any time now, so she waited.

Patricia arrived a few minutes later and told Jill that her dad had changed the locks, and that she wasn't allowed on the premises. Jill was speechless. She didn't know what to say. Patricia told her how sorry she was—but she couldn't do anything about it. Richard would have her things boxed up and sent to her. She also told her that she had better leave, because Richard had said something about hoping to run into her.

Patricia gave Jill a quick hug and told her goodbye. Again, she apologized.

"It's not your fault," Jill said, and left in a daze.

* * *

Family members can spend years seeing each other every day, eating, laughing, talking, and even sleeping together. They can also spend that many years away from one another. Then, all of a sudden, without notice, something tragic happens. Then, wherever the family members are, whatever they are doing, they come together. It's as if they all meet on the large scales of justice. Some will congregate on the right side, some on the left side. Some who don't know which side to go to will eventually just fall off into the middle. It seemed that this family was destined to be forever separated by Janyce's death. Only time would tell.

TWENTY-SEVEN

Jill still had a hard time accepting the investigation into her mother's death as closed, and Richard wasn't charged with anything. Since she was unsuccessful in getting any answers from anyone in the family, she decided to go down to the Aurora Police Department and obtain a copy of the police report.

Jill took it home with her and read it over several times. It wasn't making sense to her. She wondered what the detective was thinking. Did she believe that Richard caused her mother's death, or did she believe her mother had committed suicide? The report was sketchy. Detective Lovato had closed the case without stating her final thoughts. She didn't call Janyce's death a suicide. She didn't call it a result of natural causes, and she didn't say it was foul play. In fact, the report stated no signs of foul play. Jill wanted to know how the case could be closed when they didn't even rule on how her mom died.

With the report in hand, she went back down to the Aurora Police Department and demanded to speak with the Chief of Police. She was determined to get some answers. In her mind, the case was not closed and wouldn't be until she knew for sure how her mom died. The police chief told her the investigation into her mother's death was closed. The detectives were off the case, and they had been instructed not to speak with anyone further about it. He put his hand on Jill's shoulder, and with a stern nod, told her to stay out of this business. She didn't know what she was getting herself into, he said, and she needed to leave it alone.

Jill felt defeated. What else could she do? She went home wishing she could have been stronger and more knowledgeable, so she could have dealt with the situation better. That conversation and how she handled herself would haunt her for years to come.

* * *

Jill moved in with her boyfriend, Mark St. George, whom she met before her mom died. He was a handsome man with blond hair and blue eyes. He was smart, drove a Corvette, and owned his own business. He was also a musician. Jill went along to the gigs he booked and enjoyed watching him play while she danced along to the music.

She wanted to start working as a nail artist again and thought it would be a good idea to work out of their house. When she called Patricia to ask if she would return her supplies, Patricia said that they were hiring two new employees. Jill doubted The Nail Affaire would be in business much longer. She was the one who, besides having a long list of her own clients, took care of running the salon, processing credit cards and taking care of bookkeeping.

It seemed like Richard and his kids just did whatever they damn well pleased, no matter who they hurt. For years he had done what he wanted to her, then he took her mom away from her, and his daughters took and kept everything that her mom owned. Jill wasn't allowed to have anything that had belonged to her mother, not even the tiniest of keepsakes. They kept everything.

She and Mark settled into a house on the corner of Mexico and Fairfax in Aurora. In the beginning, they had fun. All that quickly changed when they introduced cocaine into their relationship. It was a mutual decision. They both wanted to make some extra money and felt that selling drugs would be an easy way to get it. Mark contacted a guy he knew in Boulder who was happy to hook them up. The drugs quickly turned their lives around, but not in the way they had planned. The cocaine soon took control of them, and they started doing too much.

Mark quit working, and they argued about money. Then he started to abuse Jill, not only physically, but sexually and emotionally as well. She was becoming so paranoid she would constantly stare through the peephole in the door and peer out the windows just waiting for the police to come and bust them. It was to the point where she actually prayed they would come so she could put an end to the nightmare.

Then she discovered that she was pregnant. The minute she found out, she quit. Jill loved her unborn child and felt that her being pregnant would have a positive effect on Mark. She was wrong. If anything, their relationship got worse. He continued doing cocaine, and sometimes he would leave the house and be gone for two to four days at a time. Jill would always stay home and wait for him to return.

She got another job to help make ends meet and worked at a mortgage company as a shipper during the day. On Saturdays, she continued to do nails. It was hard for her to take care of herself and keep her mind on work when she was always worried about where Mark was and what he was doing.

When she was a few months pregnant, they decided to get married. For a short time, she was happy. She felt that Mark was finally ready to settle down and be a husband and father. The day they got married, he took her to California for their honeymoon. One of Jill's old high school boyfriends worked at a hotel and arranged for them to stay there free, along with a complimentary rental car.

They had very little money to spend on their honeymoon. Mark took his pregnant new wife to the local bar. Jill hated it. She really didn't want to be in a smoke-filled dive with a bunch of drunks. He knew she wouldn't drink while she was pregnant.

After being there for a few hours, Jill was ready to go, but he wasn't. He instructed his new bride to drive the rental car back to the hotel. She drove back to the hotel, took a long bath, and dressed in the sexy lingerie she had brought for her special night. Then she settled into bed to wait for her new husband. He never returned. Finally, she fell into a restless sleep.

The sun came up, and still no Mark. He finally strolled in around nine. Jill confronted him, and he said he had met a girl in the bar. She was suicidal, so he had no choice but to go home with her to keep her from certain death. Mark also told Jill that on his way back to the hotel, he stopped at a gas station and spent the little bit of money they had left on Lotto tickets, hoping to hit it big. Jill was angry but kept quiet to keep the confrontation from escalating. If she did yell at him, it would cause a big fight, and Mark would leave her there alone.

Now she was faced with the embarrassment and shame of having to call her Uncle Ted. She had no choice, though, and Ted agreed to wire them the money, but not before giving her a stern lecture. He told her how irresponsible she and Mark were and went on to say they more or less threw away the money that they received for their wedding. He asked if they had nothing better to do than to take last-minute plane trips and buy lottery tickets, not to mention they had a baby on the way. Before Jill got off the phone, she thanked him and promised to repay him.

TWENTY-EIGHT

Not long after Janyce died, life started to spiral downward for Richard. His businesses began losing money. Construction of new properties was at a standstill. Tenants were moving out of his rental units. It seemed that Richard Hansen Enterprises was quickly becoming a thing of the past. His losses could very well have been the result of Denver sinking into a depression, due to the price drop of crude oil.

During the 1980s, Denver was losing population and was experiencing the highest office vacancy rate in the nation. That may have been a contributing factor in his losing business. At the time, he didn't realize that may be the case, so he put the blame on Janyce's family for his losses.

In May of 1985, he filed a lawsuit against Molly and Helen for one million dollars for defamation of character. He claimed that they had gone all over Denver telling anyone who would listen that Richard killed his wife. As a direct result of their actions, he was losing a large amount of money, he claimed. The case was later settled in Richard's favor, and in March of 1986, a judgment was entered against Helen and Molly in the amount of three hundred eighty-five dollars each. To this date, the judgment has not been satisfied.

Over the course of the next year and a half, Richard spent a lot of time in and out of courts for a number of different reasons. If he wasn't suing someone, they were suing him. The police were also watching him. Even though they didn't have enough to warrant an arrest for his involvement in Janyce's death, they kept a close eye on him.

With Janyce out of the picture, Richard's lifestyle didn't have to change at all. In fact, he found it was easier to do whatever he wanted, whenever he wanted to do it. He didn't have to come up with any more excuses or lies. He didn't have to come home earlier or quit drinking. He was free to indulge in all the sex, carousing, partying, corruption, and anything else he wanted to do.

The Empire Bath club was among his favorite places to frequent. Eye witnesses report that he showed no discretion when finding a companion to accompany him home. It has been said that often he would bring home one of the men he went to visit at the club. He also hopped from bar to bar picking up women and taking them home.

One evening out, he met Darla* and Ivy*, two beautiful young women, and brought them home that night. Soon thereafter, they moved into Richard's house, where they continued to live over the next several months with his daughter Patricia and son David. He referred to his new playmates as The Maids.

For the first seventeen months after Janyce's death, Richard was arrested four times. The charges ranged from DUIs, possession of dangerous drugs and failing to appear. His driver's license was eventually suspended due to a DUI, but that didn't deter him from getting another one, and he continued to drive himself around.

On the afternoon of October 1, 1986, Officer Day was called to the driver's license station on Havana Street in Aurora. A male subject was attempting to obtain a Colorado driver's license using a false birth certificate. Officer Day responded and arrested the suspect for criminal impersonation and forgery. It was Patricia's boyfriend, Troy*. He was driving a white 1976 Corvette registered to Richard Hansen.

Richard arrived to claim his vehicle and produced a Colorado ID card for identification. Upon further checking, the officer discovered that Richard's driver's license had been suspended.

A few weeks later, on the evening of November 19, 1986, Officer Day was on routine patrol on South Havana Street when he noticed a black 1980 Porsche with Colorado plates A-II. The vehicle turned into a parking lot, and Officer Day noticed that Richard was driving. The officer waited for him to leave the parking lot, then followed and stopped the car.

When Richard exited the car, Officer Day asked, "Could I see your license and registration, sir?"

Richard produced a valid Colorado Driver's License in the name of Richard Machiavelli, date of birth as 6/01/1944, and a registration for the car in the same name. The officer looked at it and said, "Is your name Richard Machiavelli?"

Richard replied, "Yes."

"Have you ever gone by a different name?" the officer asked.

"No."

"The last time I had contact with you, you stated that your name was Richard Hansen, and Richard Hansen's driver's license is suspended," the officer said.

"That wasn't me," Richard replied.

Knowing full well that he was lying, Officer Day arrested Richard and had his car towed to the Aurora Police Department impound lot.

Once at the police department, Richard said that his license had previously been suspended for points, and he was given a restricted red license. Awhile after that, he was arrested for driving under the influence and driving using his restricted license. He was found guilty in Denver County Court, at which time his license was again suspended.

Richard went on to say that after looking through the telephone directory and finding no one under the name of Richard Machiavelli, he assumed that identity. He did it for the sole purpose of obtaining a valid driver's license, so he could drive without being fearful of being stopped under suspension. Should he be stopped for a traffic violation using the Richard Machiavelli license, then he would basically have a clean slate.

After they verified that Richard Machiavelli and Richard Hansen were one in the same, they released Richard on bond. Shirley*, his girlfriend at the time, posted the three thousand dollar cash bond and took Richard home to his house on Cedar Avenue.

Two days after his arrest, he returned to the Aurora Police Department to obtain a release for his Porsche, which had been towed. After obtaining the release, he went to the tow company on Buckley Road to retrieve it. Then he got behind the wheel and drove away. Not long after that, Officer Simms observed him driving and stopped him. He issued Richard two tickets, one for driving under suspension, and one for not having proof of insurance. Simms then told Detective Bennett what had transpired.

Detective Bennett contacted Richard at his office and asked him to bring the copy of the summons he had just received down to the Aurora Police Department. That summons would then be voided, and Detective Bennett would add an additional count of Driving under suspension to his case. Richard did what the detective asked.

In all, he was charged with Criminal Impersonation, two counts of Driving Under Suspension, Unlawful Use of License, and Obtaining a False License While Under Suspension.

On January 21, 1987, he pled guilty to a false statement on a driver's license and Driving Under Suspension. The other charges were dismissed. Richard was sentenced to thirty days work release, one day PSC and fines and court costs.

* * *

Twenty-three years later, John found out that his dad had used the name, Richard Machiavelli. Niccolo Machiavelli, an Italian statesman and famous author, was known for his claim that a prince has to be deceitful if it is necessary and suits his purpose. He should also be feared, rather than loved by people.

In the 1960s, the labels of Machiavellian or Machiavellistic could be affixed to anything that was considered wrong or inhumane. Machiavellianism is also the term some social psychologists use to describe a person's tendency to deceive and manipulate others for personal gain.

Johnny received a copy of police documents that revealed his dad had several different credit cards under his assumed name. Attached to the police report was a copy of a notarized Power of Attorney signed by Richard Machiavelli dated November 20, 1986 authorizing Richard R. Hansen, representing R. R. H. Trust, to sign any and all documents pertaining to the transfer of his dad's Mercedes Benz and Porsche, with personalized plates, #A-I and A-II.

It was obvious that his dad must have been up to something. Perhaps it was the rumored position he held with organized crime. An individual who shall remain anonymous told Johnny during the research and writing of this book that Richard was the captain of the Italian Mafia and was given the name Richard Machiavelli. The person also warned Johnny to never disclose his source.

TWENTY-NINE

In September of 1986, Jill gave birth to a beautiful baby boy, whom Mark and she named Travis. Her mom had always told her that if she and Mark had babies, they would be beautiful. She was saddened that her mother couldn't be there to share the joy and love she felt for her new son. It broke her heart that Travis would never be able to meet his beautiful grandmother.

Jill couldn't spend as much time with Travis as she would have liked because she was still working two jobs. Mark wouldn't change diapers, and he spent a lot of time drinking.

A friend of Jill's had recently married a very wealthy man, and she invited Jill to stay at their house. It would only be temporary, a few weeks at best, while they were out of town. Jill was thankful for any chance that would get her away from Mark. She would have time to clear her head and figure out what to do about her sham of a marriage.

She and Travis moved into the beautiful home, and Jill had full use of everything, including her friend's car. She continued to work at a nail shop, while a friend babysat Travis. Once in a while her friend would keep him overnight. On those evenings, Jill would forget she was married and had a baby and host naked hot tub parties for her friends. Everyone attending would stay until all hours of the morning, talking and drinking.

After a few weeks, Jill realized this wasn't the answer to her problems. She felt if she was living with Mark, she could provide a more stable environment for Travis. Maybe Mark had come to the realization that having his wife and son around wouldn't be so bad. So she moved back home only to find that her husband's abusive behavior continued, and he was still playing games. Nothing had changed in the least.

* * *

December, 1986. Over the last couple years since his mom's death, Johnny had spent his time in the service. After completing his time at Fort Stewart, Georgia, he was sent to Korea, where he served for fourteen months before being released. On December 22, 1986, he was reassigned to the United States Army Separation Transfer Point in San Francisco and would be sent home to Denver. He had kept in touch with his dad by phone during the many months he was in Korea and called him to let him know he was coming home. After he hung up the phone, Johnny couldn't help but wonder what life would be like back in Denver now that his mom was gone.

He had received a letter from his sister Jill, who told him that Auntie Helen and Uncle Ted had hired an attorney for him, Jaqueline, and herself. The attorney was retained to help find their mother's safety deposit boxes and make sure the three of them were not cheated out of what was rightfully theirs. The boxes were eventually discovered, but they were empty. So whatever their mother wanted them to have had conveniently disappeared.

Richard had been able to obtain access to her safety deposit box, and when he appeared for a deposition, stated that the only items in the box were stocks, which were in his name only. If Janyce did have a will, or any life insurance policies, they were never found.

Jill also wrote Johnny that Richard had warned her to never step foot on the property and had kept her from working at The Nail Affaire.

Johnny planned to attend the Community College of Aurora and get his Associate of Arts Degree. He was sure his dad would put him to work. In the past, he had worked for him at the properties he owned and rented out. Johnny, along with Richard's other kids, would help shovel sidewalks, mow lawns, paint, and do general maintenance work. Once in a while, his dad would even have him collect the rent from various tenants. Now that he was twenty-four and out of the army, maybe his dad would assign him a position at Richard Hansen Enterprises. Then he'd be set for life. Having a job and money would never be a problem for him again. He would have the world at his feet, just like his dad.

He arrived in Denver around midnight, expecting his dad to be at the airport to pick him up. When he didn't show up in an hour, Johnny wasn't that surprised and called his old girlfriend, Gloria. Luckily he could still count on her. She picked him up at the airport, and he spent the night at her place. One night led to another, and he ended up moving in with her.

He had a hard time trying to figure out what to do with his life. It's not as if he could just pick up where he left off. If his mom were still alive, he would be able to sit down with her and have a long heart-to-heart, as they had done so many times in the past. She would guide him in the right direction and bring a sense of purpose and belonging back into his life. But with his mom gone, Johnny was on his own.

* * *

He attended college during the day and worked at night and on the weekends as his dad's personal chauffer. At the time, Richard owned three different Mercedes. Johnny thought he was pretty hot when he got behind the wheel of one of those, and he was enjoying his job.

On the weekends, he drove his dad around to various locations so he could check on his different properties and collect rent. In the evenings, he would take him to the different discos and nightclubs and then drive him home. On occasion, his dad invited Johnny to join him as he partied the night away.

One of their favorite hangouts was NEO's, an upscale dance club in Glendale located off Alameda near Colorado Boulevard. The club adhered to a strict dress code. In the lower level, was the Piranha Room, a small, very exclusive, member's only, discothèque. The furniture was retro-modern. The theme was a razor-tooth graphic of a vicious fish grinding its jaws. Johnny would stay upstairs at NEO's and party with his friends while his dad headed downstairs to the Piranha Room.

The room quickly earned the reputation of being the wildest bar in the Denver metro area. It became notorious for sex and drugs. Club members had bags of cocaine. The doorman sold Ecstasy. Richard and the other members would drink excessively on top of all the drugs they did. They used the lobby phones to dial phone sex, while others were having sex in the bathrooms, in the corners, and in the parking lot.

There were many nights that his dad wanted to keep the party going when they arrived home from the bars. Richard's on again-off again girlfriend, Shirley, lived in her own apartment, and Darla and Ivy, The Maids, still lived at his dad's house. Johnny liked hanging out with the two girls. Often, his friends, Matt and Kevin, partied with them. Johnny felt a twinge of pain when he saw his dad having so much fun. He still had a hard time dealing with his mom's death, and it hurt to see his dad so happy with other women. Johnny made those thoughts disappear as he belted down another drink.

He felt his relationship with Gloria had turned more into a convenience for him than anything else. For her, it was another story. Johnny was starting to feel her resentment toward him. He couldn't blame her when one day she told him to pack up and move out.

The Maids had moved out of Richard's house, so his old room was empty. Johnny's dad gave him the okay to move back in. As each day passed, he was starting to feel more and more like this was his home again. He had been away for so long that it was hard to get comfortable, especially around his dad. Their relationship had always been strained, to say the least; but each day brought them closer together. Johnny actually started to feel a father-son bond growing between them.

One afternoon, he was driving his dad over to Niles' office near Peoria and Chambers. On the drive, they had been reminiscing about the past.

Richard said, "You know what, Johnny? I don't think many young men at the age of twenty-three can say that they have driven as many luxury cars as you have."

"Don't I know it" Johnny replied, "especially one that belonged to Helen Reddy. Man that was so cool driving that back to Denver. It was even cooler being in her mansion. I can't believe she had a bowling alley in her basement."

His dad had responded to an ad in the paper and made arrangements to buy the singer's Rolls Royce Cornice for around one hundred grand. Richard had Johnny and David fly out to her home in Beverly Hills and drive the Rolls Royce back to Colorado. It was a beauty, a white convertible with red leather interior. While looking at it, she asked them to please disregard the scratches on the interior. They were caused by her dog. Johnny smiled and thought, *Okay Helen, you're the star, and you're asking us to please do something?* He thought she was so cool. The brothers left, and Johnny drove the Rolls Royce from California straight back to Denver.

Still, something was not quite right about the whole deal. He couldn't figure out why his dad wanted him to drive such an expensive car home. Johnny was only sixteen years old at the time and had just got his driver's license. He didn't have much experience behind the wheel, and he had to drive through the mountains no less. Maybe his dad was hoping he would pile it up so he could collect the insurance money. That scenario seemed to fit with what really happened. While Johnny was away in the service, the Rolls Royce, apparently, got stolen. After that, it was rumored in the family that Richard arranged to have someone steal it. The car was never recovered, and Richard collected the insurance money.

Finally Johnny felt comfortable enough to ask his dad the question that had been eating away at him for over two years. As he was pulling up to Niles' office, he looked over at him and said, "Dad. What really happened to Mom? Did you kill her like everyone said?"

The moment he saw the look in his dad's eyes, he regretted saying it and thought he might kill him right then and there. Instead, Richard took his elbow and crammed it into Johnny's side as hard as he could.

Through clenched teeth, he said, "Don't you ever say anything like that again, or even mention that word ever."

Wincing in pain and still trying to catch his breath, Johnny pulled into a parking space at the office complex, put the car into park, and turned off the engine. Richard opened up his car door, and while getting out of the passenger side, he told Johnny to wait in the car and then slammed the door.

Johnny sat there waiting for his dad to return and regretting what he had said. Now he had spoiled whatever chance he may have had with building a relationship with him. But he also thought about his mother. He needed to know what really happened. Although he didn't know any more than before, he would always be able to console himself with the fact that at least he had asked his dad.

THIRTY

Early in spring of 1987, Richard announced to Johnny that he was moving to Puerto Vallarta, Mexico. Johnny wasn't surprised by his decision to move out of the country. He had mentioned it before. He'd been doing things out of the ordinary lately, and he seemed to be depressed, moody, losing weight, and sleeping more than usual. Johnny tried to get him out of his slump by offering to take him bar hopping a few times, but his dad declined.

Maybe he was going through a mid-life crisis or something. He had just turned fifty-five and had a hard time accepting the fact that he was getting older. It became obvious to Johnny when he found out that one of his dad's driver's licenses showed him to be only forty-nine. His Richard Machiavelli license showed his age as forty-three.

Richard moved to Puerto Vallarta and left his on again-off again girlfriend, Shirley, behind. He had long since gotten rid of The Maids. Richard just came home one day with a new girlfriend and announced she was moving in, so the other two had to go. Johnny wondered why his dad let Shirley stay living at the house when he moved to Mexico. She was a little dingy and young enough to be his dad's daughter. But he rarely saw her. Between college and his job delivering airline tickets to various businesses around Denver, he kept himself busy.

His dad often wrote him long thoughtful letters describing what his life was like living on the beach in Mexico. He sent Johnny pictures he had taken of seagulls and pelicans in flight. Johnny was relieved. He had been worried about his dad's health before he left. Now, he seemed to be in good spirits.

They often called each other just to talk and were actually building a good rapport through their phone conversations. Richard apologized to Johnny for being so hard on him in the past, and said that as a father he had done many things he regretted. He expressed deep sorrow over Janyce's death and told Johnny how much he missed having her in his life. Johnny had accepted the fact that his mother committed suicide.

In one letter, his dad told him to quit smoking pot.

"There is no way anyone can function too
well while on pot… Please don't call me when
you're high or loaded, you are too difficult to
understand… Try to stop saying 'okay' and
'yup' and 'alright' when you talk to people, it's
bad grammar and confusing to listen to."

In the letter, he suggested Johnny take speaking classes, as Richard had taken the Dale Carnegie classes. He signed the letter, "Love, Dad."

* * *

One evening Richard phoned and said he was no longer content to just sit on his balcony and watch the birds fly by. He had looked into different investments in Mexico, but nothing appealed to him. So he suggested to Johnny that he look around Denver for some sort of business opportunity they could get into together. Johnny was excited, because he and Seth had already been discussing the possibility of opening a car wash. He told his dad about their idea, and Richard thought it was a good one. He told Johnny to do the research, and he would back them all the way.

Johnny and Seth wanted to open three car washes, each at a different location. They looked at property, profits, and high traffic areas, and Johnny kept his dad abreast of their plans, talking to him daily. When he said that he had the final prospectus ready, his dad announced that he was moving back to Aurora.

When his dad arrived home, Johnny couldn't be happier. Richard was eager to get the car wash business set up with him and said he'd always wanted Johnny to be a part of Richard Hansen Enterprises. That was his ultimate goal from the time he set him up in college. By Johnny getting his degree and then becoming an architect, he could design the company's commercial and residential properties.

Just when they were ready to start the financing on the car washes, Johnny was called up for a two-week bivouac in Alaska for the Army Reserves. As eager as they were to get the business going, Richard wanted to wait for him to return before beginning the finance process. He wanted Johnny to be involved in every aspect of getting their project up and running.

* * *

On Father's Day, 1987, Johnny had been in Alaska for a little over a week. He placed a call to his dad and learned that he was in the hospital. Alarmed, he called him there.

Richard answered the phone. "Hey, Johnny, I was just thinking about you. How's it going in Alaska?"

"Everything is going fine," he replied. "What's going on with you? Why are you in the hospital?"

"I just have a touch of pneumonia. I should be out of here in plenty of time to pick you up at the airport when you arrive home."

"Well Dad," he said, "I just wanted to call you quick and wish you a happy Father's Day. Get yourself better, and I'll see you when I get home. I can hardly wait to get our deal underway."

"Thank you, son. I can hardly wait for you to get home, as well. I miss having you around. I have really enjoyed your company lately. Before you hang up, I just want you to know how proud I am of you. I love you, Johnny. Goodbye."

"Bye, Dad," he replied. "I love you too."

* * *

On the Saturday morning of June 27, 1987, Jill was up early after a restless night. Mark had left the previous evening and still hadn't returned home. The phone rang, and she felt a sinking feeling as she went to answer. She thought it might be Mark offering up some pathetic excuse as to why he hadn't come home all night. Instead, a rather cheerful Auntie Helen was on the line. She told Jill that she was calling to inform her that Richard had died yesterday. Helen went on to give her the details of his death, telling Jill she heard the news from their cousin who worked at the hospital.

When Jill hung up the phone, just for a moment, she was in a state of shock. Then she reached down, and swooping up Travis, she started doing a happy dance around the room. "Daddy Dicky's dead," she sang. "We're going to go dance and spit on his grave. Daddy Dicky's dead."

After dancing around the room, Jill sat down and cradled her son in her arms. Tears came to her eyes as she looked down at her little boy and thanked God he would never know the man who had caused her so much pain. Jill smiled as she thought to herself *how ironic and what a fitting way for the bastard to die.*

* * *

The days in Alaska didn't go quickly enough for Johnny, but now he was finished and going home. His plane arrived in Colorado Springs, Colorado. No one was there to pick him up. Once again, he was faced with wondering how he would get home. He called his dad and a few friends he thought could pick him up but was unable to reach anyone. He happened to run into a fellow reserves man who had been on the plane with him, and he offered to give Johnny a ride home to Denver.

It was dark when they arrived at the house on Cedar Avenue. Johnny invited the reserves man in for a drink before he left. They both got out of the car. Johnny stood there a moment looking at the house. It was pitch black, and everything seemed so still. He had a strange sense of foreboding that something was wrong. The eerie feeling continued as he walked in the darkness to the front door. It was locked. He found the spare key they kept hidden outside for emergencies, unlocked the door, and slowly opened it. He reached for the switch, and light filled the room as Johnny looked around. Everything seemed to be in place.

After walking through the house, he discovered that no one was home. That was strange. Usually someone was always there. If not, at least a light was left on. Johnny called his Nanny to see if she knew where his dad was.

She answered on the first ring, and he could tell immediately that something was wrong. "Hi, Nanny. It's me Johnny. What's going on?"

As she spoke, her words were practically incoherent. "I have frantically been trying to reach you, Johnny. I have bad news. You know your father was in the hospital with pneumonia. We all thought he was feeling better, but he took a turn for the worst."

"I know," he said. "I spoke with him on Father's Day. Try to stop crying, Nanny. I can hardly understand what you are saying. Calm down and tell me what's wrong."

"Your dad died yesterday," she sobbed.

"No," he shouted. The world went black around him, and he collapsed onto the floor.

* * *

A somber Johnny attended his father's funeral, with just as much dignity and respect as he had shown at his mother's funeral. Johnny was numb. He just buried his mother less than three years ago, and now his father.

Richard had served his country as a Private in the United States Marine Corps, and was honored with a military funeral on July 1, 1987. Interment was held at Fort Logan Cemetery in Denver, Colorado.

Johnny later learned that his dad had contracted Acquired *Immuno*deficiency Syndrome (AIDS), which led to pneumonia. Richard was admitted to St. Anthony's Central Hospital in Denver, Colorado soon after Johnny had left for his two-week bivouac in Alaska. On June 24, 1987, Richard was transferred to the Department of Veterans Affairs Hospital in Denver, Colorado, where he died.

The first AIDS cases reported were in 1981. The number of cases and deaths increased rapidly in the 1980s, the greatest impact of the epidemic being among men who have sex with men. No one knows when Richard became aware that he was infected or how many people, both male and female, he may have infected.

THIRTY-ONE

A few months had passed since Richard's death. Johnny still lived at his father's house, as did Patricia and Richard's girlfriend, Shirley. He wondered why she was still there. Her boyfriend was dead, and she was still hanging around. Oh well. He really didn't care one way or the other. Sooner or later someone would come along and boot her out. It would probably be Niles or possibly Poppy.

Johnny didn't know for sure whether or not his father left a will, but he assumed he had. After all, his dad had been a very successful businessman and owned millions in real estate. Then again, he could be wrong. He had thought his mother left one too. He'd heard that his mother's estate transferred to his dad. Either way, with both parents deceased, he was sure he would receive his equal share of his dad's estate, along with his other siblings. Johnny didn't really dwell on the fact that someday he would have a lot of money. He wasn't one to sit idly by and wait for his ship to come in. When he wasn't attending college or enlisted in the service, he always had a job, and he wasn't afraid to work.

When he was sixteen, his dad had taught him a very valuable lesson. Johnny was in his bedroom putting money in his dresser drawer when his dad came in and asked him where he got it. The drawer was filled with hundreds of one dollar bills, fives and tens. There was almost a thousand dollars. Johnny replied that he had earned it from work, and he had been saving it.

"You have a good start," he said. "You have to have money to make money. Get that money in that bank and I will match it dollar-for-dollar as long as you keep saving."

Johnny saved every dollar he earned, and true to his word, his dad matched it all. Soon he had enough to buy his first car, a blue Volkswagen Bug. His buddy, Kevin, had a white bug, and Matt had a red one. Those days were crazy fun for Johnny and his friends. The three of them would drive their little cars around like maniacs.

Suffering the loss of both parents in the span of just two and a half years was tough. Johnny did what he knew best. He continued his college education at the Aurora Community College and was still enlisted with the Army Reserves. He also landed a part-time job at the local pizza parlor and continued to party every chance he got.

Among his favorite places to go was still the local hot spot, NEO's with its exclusive Piranha Room. Johnny liked to go to the club on Thursdays because it was ladies night. On this particular Thursday night, September 24, 1987, he was walking around the top level of the club when a tall, leggy blonde caught his eye. He watched her from across the room as she talked to her friend. He liked the way she smiled. In fact, he liked everything about her. He deliberately walked by and looked at her, and she looked back at him. He knew then and there he had to meet her. He circled the club then approached her and engaged her in a conversation.

Her name was Kim. She worked for an oil and gas law firm as a legal assistant in Aurora. He also noticed the key she was holding was for a Porsche. They discovered they would both be celebrating their birthdays in the next couple of days. Kim would be turning thirty-one on Friday, and Johnny would be turning twenty-five on Saturday. Kim had to get up early the next morning for work, so after assuring each other they would meet again, they wished each other Happy Birthday, and said their goodbyes. Kim and her girlfriend left the club.

A couple days had passed. It was Saturday night. Johnny and Kim were each celebrating their birthdays with a few of their friends at NEO's when they ran into each other again. Johnny didn't waste any time and asked her to dance. Kim accepted, and as Johnny took off his tailored suit coat, she noticed that he had a pack of cigarettes in his front breast pocket of his shirt.

She immediately thought to herself, *Yuck. He smokes.* Kim also felt

Johnny was too young for her, but it was just a dance. Putting those two issues aside, she liked what she saw. He seemed very intelligent and quite the gentleman. He certainly had a sense of style, dressing in tailored suits and ties. Last, but not least, he was handsome.

As the two danced, it was obvious they liked each other. At that time, Johnny may not have known where their attraction to each other would lead, but Kim did. As she watched Johnny dance, an aura seemed to surround him. She had an overwhelming feeling that this wasn't just a dance, and one day, Johnny would become her husband. Kim was surprised by her feelings because she had just gone through a divorce a year earlier, and getting serious about anyone had been the last thing on her mind.

When the bar closed, they decided to go somewhere for breakfast. Kim's best friend, whose name was also Kim, had ridden to NEO's with her earlier that evening. So the girls went in Kim's Porsche to the restaurant, while Johnny followed in his car. After eating Johnny and Kim exchanged phone numbers and said their goodbyes. Not long after the two Kims got home, the phone rang. Kim H. was closest to the phone, so she answered it. It was a male caller, and he asked to speak with Kim. Not giving it a thought as to who was calling, or which Kim he wanted to speak to, Kim H. replied, "This is Kim."

It was Johnny. He was very intoxicated and commenced to spilling his guts to Kim H. He talked for over an hour about the deaths of both of his parents and the effect it was having on his life. Kim listened in on the conversation, not wanting to announce herself as the Kim he really wanted to talk to because Kim H. had already been the one who was doing the talking.

During the conversation, Johnny asked her to go with him to a hockey game. Kim shook her head no, so Kim H. declined the offer for her. Kim didn't want to date anyone at the time. She felt sympathy for what Johnny was going through, as she had felt the pain of losing her mother just a few years earlier.

He continued calling and asking her out. He even sent flowers to her office. Still she kept putting him off. She liked Johnny, but she felt he was too young for her. She just turned thirty-one, and he was only twenty-five. Maybe her sixth sense was right, and she would marry him one day. But for now she was going to keep her distance.

Yet they continued to run into each other at NEO's. Kim H. was always with Kim. Johnny nicknamed the two Kims "double trouble."

The three became good friends and would dance the night away, closing down the bars, then go out to breakfast. Kim hosted several Sunday afternoon Bronco parties, which Johnny attended, as a friend. He offered to help cook or clean up and was always the perfect gentleman. But he wouldn't give up trying to convince Kim that she should go out with him. He continued calling her every day, pleading with her to go on an official date.

In November 1987, Kim finally agreed. They went to a Colorado Rangers game together. A few days later, the day before Thanksgiving, Kim received word that her father (also named Richard) had died in his sleep of a massive heart attack. Johnny wanted to accompany her to Minnesota for her father's funeral. Although he was staying at Kim's house on occasion, he still lived at his dad's house on Cedar Avenue. Kim went with Johnny to his house to get clothes for the funeral.

Her first meeting with his sister, Patricia, didn't go well. It was 5:30 a.m. Thanksgiving morning. Patricia was sleeping at the house. When Johnny woke her to tell her he was going to Minnesota with Kim to attend her father's funeral, Patricia became angry. She felt because it was Thanksgiving, Johnny should be with his Nanny and Poppy and their family for the holiday, not heading out of state to some funeral.

The trip to Minnesota brought Johnny and Kim closer together. When they returned to Colorado, they continued dating, Johnny still living at his dad's house, and Kim in her two-bedroom apartment.

THIRTY-TWO

In December 1987, tragedy again struck the Hansens. Johnny's grandparents, Poppy and Nanny, went on a short drive to visit a friend. When they arrived, Poppy didn't feel like going into the house, so he stayed in the car. Nanny was only going in for a short time, so she turned off the car and wrapped an afghan around Poppy so he would stay warm. Apparently, Poppy was smoking and dropped his cigarette. Before anyone noticed anything, the whole afghan that covered him was in flames. His entire body was burned.

Johnny and Kim went to visit him in the burn unit at University Hospital in Denver and were shocked to see that only his eyes were visible. He was wrapped like a mummy from head to toe. Johnny was devastated. He drove Kim back to her apartment, dropped her off and went on a two-day drinking binge.

He ended up at NEO's. After spending hours there, he decided it was time to go. He went to get his coat, and the coat-check girl, seeing how inebriated he was, told him not to drive. Finally, she called the police, and Johnny ended up in jail.

While he was on a bender, Poppy died and was buried. Johnny held on to even more guilt feelings after that. The fact that he let the family down by not being able to attend his grandfather's funeral was hard enough to handle.

Poppy's death seemed suspicious to the police and, of course, Nanny was questioned about it. Although the rumors were flying that maybe Nanny was somehow involved, Poppy's death was ruled accidental. Not everyone believed it.

* * *

December 24, 1987. Johnny invited Kim to attend Christmas Eve dinner with him, along with his dad's side of the family at his older sister Linda's house. Other than receiving a letter from Jill while he was in the Army, Johnny still hadn't spoken to his mom's side of the family since Janyce's funeral. Although, it was a solemn affair at Linda's without Richard and Poppy, everyone got along well and welcomed Kim into the family. Almost everyone was present except Johnny's brother, David, who was still in prison for robbing a local bank. Johnny felt somewhat sorry for him. After all, he got the hell beat out of him by Richard just as much, if not more, than Johnny had.

On Christmas Day, he took Kim to The Christiana, his dad's townhouse in Breckenridge. Johnny skied while Kim hung out at the lodge and the local shops. To add to their fun, Denver ended up getting a blizzard with thirty-five inches of snow. The interstates were closed, and the couple had to stay at the townhouse a few days longer. This was great news for Johnny, as he had fallen deeply in love with Kim and welcomed any excuse to be with her.

* * *

In March of 1988, he officially moved in with Kim into her two-bedroom apartment. Three months later, Kim's sixteen-year-old niece and her boyfriend from Wisconsin came to visit Kim for a week during summer vacation. Johnny decided to take all of them up to his dad's townhouse in Breckenridge to stay for a few days.

It wasn't long after they returned to Denver that Johnny heard through the grapevine that his dad's house on Cedar Avenue was going into foreclosure. Since living with Kim, he hadn't bothered to go back there. He decided to drive over to the house to see if he could find out any further information.

When he arrived, the house appeared as if no one had lived there for a while. It looked as if he had walked in on the middle of a burglary. He discovered that items had been removed from the house including furniture, beds, décor and most of his dad's personal items.

Lights and plumbing fixtures were gone, even bricks from around the swimming pool. His dad's cars were absent, but that was no surprise. His brother Niles had taken them right after his dad died.

Johnny quickly left and went home to tell Kim about his discovery. They surmised that if his dad or his dad's estate was bankrupt, then most likely the house was allowed to go into foreclosure. But why would his dad's estate be bankrupt? If that were the case, Johnny's brothers and sisters must be taking anything and everything. He asked Kim and her niece if they would go back to the house with him to help get a few things. They agreed and left, hoping all the while not to run into any of his family while they were there.

Although the house had been emptied of almost all of its possessions, Johnny was lucky enough to get a few items. He took an encyclopedia set that had been in the family since he was a young boy, some casual flatware, and a beautiful handmade chess set, the size of a coffee table, with two matching benches that had belonged to his mom and dad. They had purchased the set during a family vacation to Mexico several years earlier and had it shipped back to the states. Johnny knew for a fact that someone would have been back to claim it if he hadn't taken it first.

He looked around the living room, and what he saw saddened him. The house that once held all of his parents' worldly possessions, everything his mom was so proud of, was now an empty space littered with papers and empty boxes. He pictured his siblings scrounging and scurrying from room to room like rats as they took everything that they could get their hands on. A couple days after Johnny took the chess set, Patricia telephoned him saying how upset she was that he had done so. She had told Nanny and her other siblings that she wanted it, Patricia said, and they had agreed that she could have it. The conversation led to a heated argument, and Johnny refused to relinquish the set.

A couple of months later, Johnny and Kim planned to celebrate their birthdays at his dad's townhouse in Breckenridge. After everything they had been through over the last few months, they felt a weekend getaway would do them both good. Besides that, Johnny had a very important question he wanted to ask Kim. He called his sister, Kathy, and explained he would be taking Kim to the townhouse and wanted to make sure it was available. She told him that it had been sold, and all the money had gone to the bankruptcy court to settle their dad's estate. What bankruptcy court? He demanded. Why hadn't anyone told him? As they spoke, she said that there was no money left. Shocked as he was, Johnny had to focus on his life. He was planning to ask Kim to marry him, and he would have to deal with his father's estate and whatever was going on later.

He telephoned Jill. Her husband, Mark, worked for United Airlines as a baggage handler. Mark was able to get them two buddy passes on a twin-engine airplane. Saturday morning, they drove to Aspen Ski Resort. A Fall Festival was taking place on top of the mountain with live entertainment. They took a gondola ride to the top of Aspen Mountain where they ate lunch and enjoyed the music. After lunch, they walked over and sat down on a huge boulder and took in the spectacular, breathtaking views, where Johnny proposed—and Kim accepted.

They were married on November 5, 1988 at their two-story executive home they had purchased together in Aurora. Johnny's family members on his mom's side were among the sixty-plus guests. Johnny was still feuding with his dad's side of the family, so he didn't invite any of them to attend. Kim's grandparents on her father's side of the family drove in from Minnesota, and her brother and his wife also came. The wedding was held at dusk, and Kim's brother gave her away. Later, Jill told her that Grandma and the rest of the family were commenting during the ceremony how much she reminded them of Janny—not only the way she wore her hair, but because she was such a kind, loving person.

During the ceremony, Grandma Bloom kept repeating, "That bastard killed our Janny."

It bothered Kim to listen to it, and she knew Johnny must feel even worse. After all, Janyce had been dead for almost four years, and Richard had died a little over a year ago. Not that it was any easier on anyone now, but Kim felt Molly shouldn't be talking that way, especially not on Johnny's wedding day. Didn't his grandmother realize how much it hurt him to have to listen to her talk about his dad that way?

Kim soon found out that every time they were at any family gatherings, Johnny's grandmother would repeat that accusation over and over again. "That bastard killed our Janny. He killed our Janny." Auntie Helen would instruct everyone to ignore her mother when she was in that state of mind. Ever since Janyce died, Helen forbade anyone from talking about Janyce in the presence of her mother. Maybe she feared it would only antagonize the situation by making things worse, or maybe she felt her mother would have a breakdown. Whatever the reason was, no one was allowed to say anything about Janyce.

Johnny and Kim spent their honeymoon in Dillon, Colorado at Johnny's Auntie Helen and Uncle Ted's townhouse overlooking beautiful Lake Dillon. After they returned to Denver, and once the Christmas holidays were over, they would focus their attention on Richard's estate. Kathy must have assumed that Johnny would quietly walk away after she told him the money was gone. But Johnny knew a little bit about his dad's finances, and he didn't think it possible that he was broke.

THIRTY-THREE

Johnny was determined to find out for himself if his dad was bankrupt, or if he even had a will. He and Kim went to the courthouses and started digging. They found out that his dad's estate was indeed in bankruptcy, and that his dad had set up a trust.

The bankruptcy court retained seventeen different assets in all to pay debts, including the house on Cedar Avenue, several different notes on real estate, apartments, Sam Wilson's Meat Market, Mile-Hi Trailer Park, personal property, cash, back rent, all stock in Richard's companies (Diamond Hill Industries, Inc. and Richard R. Hansen, Inc.), and so on. Also, all monies held in the Registry of District Courts, including Wilson & Filteau vs. Richard Hansen, and Hansen vs. Lederman. All assets combined totaled a small fortune.

The assets retained by the R.R.H. Trust included a 500 SE Mercedes, the Smith note, and the Breckinridge townhouse, the same townhouse Kathy said had been sold to cover bankruptcy debt. According to the bankruptcy documents, they kept the proceeds from the sale of his dad's townhouse for themselves. No wonder his dad's kids were all driving new cars and moving into fancy homes. He had no idea how much they sold the townhouse for, or what the amount on the Smith note was. He hadn't seen the Mercedes around, so they probably sold that as well. He was going to find out.

Johnny wondered what could have happened to make Richard Hansen Enterprises, Inc. fall into bankruptcy. Did his Nanny and siblings have something to do with it? Were they so greedy they could only focus on the here and now? Were they only interested in getting their hands on the cash and cars? He wondered how they could be so stupid, especially Niles. How could he just walk away and forget about Richard Hansen Enterprises, Inc., something their dad had built from the ground up and kept going for over thirty years?

Johnny thought it was possible that his dad planned to go bankrupt. After all, he did have AIDS and was faced with the possibility of dying. Maybe he said to hell with it all and gave up. But that didn't make any sense either. Why accumulate all that wealth and power, only to give it up in the end? He knew his dad was a shrewd businessman. He had a sense of knowing what to do and when to do it. If nothing else, he would have at least started to liquidate all of his assets. He felt his brothers and sisters were somehow responsible for the situation. If Johnny had been in control, he wouldn't have allowed it to end this way.

* * *

He soon learned that his father had left a will dividing his estate equally among his biological children. His adopted children, Jill and Jaqueline, were to receive one dollar each. Although the will had been filed over a year ago, no one had told Johnny. His grandmother was even the Trustee of his dad's estate. It looked like no one was performing their fiduciary duties.

Apparently, Richard appointed his son Niles as his Power of Attorney on January 7, 1987. On December 1, 1987, Niles' Power of Attorney was revoked. Probably because although the Power of Attorney was executed on January 7, 1987 by Richard and Niles, and notarized by a current notary public, it wasn't recorded by the Arapahoe County Clerk until December 2, 1987. Richard Hansen was most certainly dead at the time it was recorded. This document has a handwritten note on it, apparently by the recorder, stating to return it to Richard Hansen, naming an address to send it to—which was Niles' office.

Johnny thought maybe he was wrong in placing the blame on Niles. Nanny must have been the one who had Niles' Power of Attorney revoked.

Apparently, Janyce granted Richard her Power of Attorney on a legal document, and it was notarized on March 16, 1982. It was recorded at the courthouse on November 27, 1984, a couple months after Janyce died. The exact same document, which is most certainly a copy because not so much as a letter is different in her signature, (if it was her real signature), was signed and notarized on the same date of March 16, 1982 and filed on December 3, 1987. That was a stretch since Janyce died on September 21, 1984.

So Niles' Power of Attorney for Richard was recorded December 1, 1987, and it was recorded as revoked December 2, 1987. Richard's Power of Attorney for Janyce was recorded December 3, 1987. That's the first, second, and third of December 1987. One would think the Hansens kept these notarized documents lying around until someone died. Then if someone stood to benefit from the death, the recorder at the courthouse was notified and filed each document. They were all recorded after Janyce's and Richard's deaths.

After Johnny examined Janyce's signature on the Power of Attorney, it was obvious to him that it was not anywhere near to his mother's real signature. When she died, no will was discovered, so naturally everything of hers went to Richard. Yet her name was still on the El Greco Apartment Complex Note that the bankruptcy court retained to pay debts. A former business partner of Ted's and Richard's telephoned Ted sometime after Richard's death to tell him that Janyce still owned half of the assets in the El Greco Apartments.

Armed with this new information, Helen and Ted immediately hired an attorney on behalf of Johnny, Jill, and Jaqueline. The attorney filed a claim with the U.S. Bankruptcy Court. Although Richard R. Hansen, Janyce's surviving spouse, was an heir at law of Janyce's estate (since she apparently had no will), a stipulation was approved by the U.S. Bankruptcy Court and the Arapahoe County District Court in Case No. A-87-CV-49, stating, "... the Estate of Richard R. Hansen, now deceased, will not participate in any distribution from Janyce's Estate."

On February 9, 1989, the attorney representing Janyce's Estate received a settlement check from the bankruptcy trustee in the amount of $98,843.88. Ted was reimbursed expenses he paid for Janyce's funeral, and the rest was divided equally among Johnny, Jill, and Jaqueline. Surely, Nanny was trying to cover all the bases, assuming everything that belonged to Janyce would become Richard's. This one must have gotten overlooked.

Several years later, Johnny would discover that his mother's name was also on several other notes that were listed in his dad's bankruptcy, not just the El Greco Apartment Complex. He had to wonder if his Uncle Ted and the attorney were working together. After all, they were good friends. Did they pocket money that he and his two sisters should have? At the time, why hadn't the attorney discovered Janyce's name on the other notes as well? Or did he? If he had made the discovery, then that money would have gone to Johnny, Jill, and Jaqueline.

Uncle Ted had recently told Johnny there was at least two hundred thousand in cash in the safety deposit box that his mother wanted her children to have. But of course, Richard got to it first, or so Ted said. But how would Ted know this information? During the deposition when the attorneys questioned Richard about its contents, he claimed there were only stock certificates in the safety deposit box, and they were all in his name.

Years later Johnny would also learn that about a month after Janyce died, Ted said he received a bill from the bank asking for payment on the safety deposit box that she rented. Why would he be receiving Janyce's mail? Helen told Cindy that she and Ted hired an attorney on Johnny's, Jill's, and Jaqueline's behalf to find the elusive safety deposit box. Maybe it wasn't Richard who got to it first. Could Ted and the attorney have taken the contents of the box? Would Johnny and Jill ever know the real truth?

THIRTY-FOUR

April 1989. Johnny left the courthouse knowing he had to do something. He was determined not to let Nanny and his dad's kids get away with taking everything, especially what was rightfully his. He couldn't believe the nerve of them.

On the drive home, he decided to hire the attorney at the law firm where Kim worked. Since Kim was familiar with estates and probates, she could keep Johnny abreast of everything as it transpired.

On May 11, 1989, the attorney representing Johnny sent Violet Hansen, Trustee of the R.R.H Trust, a letter stating their demands. A summary of the attorney's letter follows:

> As the trustee, Violet has failed in her duty to send a notice to Johnny, as he is a beneficiary of the trust. She has failed to keep Johnny reasonably informed of the trust. The attorney asks her to provide a complete copy of the trust with all relevant information, provide a complete accounting of the trust from its inception through present; provide a list of all transactions, distributions, present assets and liabilities; and complete details relating to the sale of the Breckenridge condominium. The attorney allows Violet ten days to respond with a satisfactory accounting and production of documents, or he will file the appropriate actions in the District Court of Denver.

* * *

For the next several months, numerous telephone calls and correspondence between Johnny's attorney and the Hansen family took place. Johnny's attorney sent another written demand to Violet Hansen.

On May 1990, Johnny's attorney received a written response, but not by Violet Hansen, the Trustee; but rather from David on behalf of the Hansen Family. Following is the (unedited) letter:

DEAR MR. CAMPBELL*

WE HAVE ATTEMPTED TO ANSWER YOUR CLIENTS ALLEGATIONS IN THE ORDER IN WHICH THEY WERE PRESENTED TO US.

1. ON OR ABOUT JULY OF 1988 VIOLET HANSEN WAS GIVEN DIRECT PERMISSION BY JOHN HANSEN TO SIGN HIS NAME TO ANY DOCUMENTS CONCERNING THE SETTLEMENT OF THE BANKRUPTCY OF RICHARD HANSEN. JOHN STATED THAT HE WOULD BE EXTREMELY DIFFICULT TO GET A HOLD OF AND THAT VIOLET HANSEN SHOULD DEFINITELY USE HER DISCRETION AND SIGN HIS NAME IF NEED BE.

2. THE TRUST/ESTATE CONSISTED OF $76,000 AND THE CONDO IN BRECKENRIDGE (WHICH SOLD FOR A PROFIT OF $25,000) TOTALLING $101,000. A PORTION OF THE 101K WAS PAID BACK TO VIOLET HANSEN FOR LEGAL EXPENSES AND MISC. EXPENSES INCURRED (SEE ATTACHED).

3. THIS ALLEGATION IS ABSURED.

4. THE BANKRUPTCY COURT HAS TAKEN OVER THE MAJORITY OF THE ASSETS ASSIGNED TO THE TRUST.

5. THE 500 SE MERCEDES BELONGS TO VIOLET HANSEN. IT'S OWNERSHIP HAS

BEEN IN HER NAME SINCE BEFORE RICHARD HANSEN'S DEATH. NILES STILL DOES NOT OWN THAT CAR.

6. THE TRUST WAS REGISTERED.

7. ALL I.R.S. FORMS HAVE BEEN FILED AND TAKEN CARE OF.

8. UNTRUE.

9. THE CONDO IN BRECKENRIDGE WAS SOLD AT A FAIR PRICE THROUGH A REALESTATE COMPANY IN THE SUMMIT COUNTY COMMUNITY.

10. AS A BENEFICIARY JOHN HANSEN HAS RECEIVED MORE THAN HIS FAIR TREATMENT FROM VIOLET HANSEN. ACCORDING TO ARTICLE ELEVENTH (NO CONTEST) AND ARTICLE 3. OF THE CODICIL OF RICHARD HANSEN'S WILL JOHN HANSEN SHOULD NOT HAVE RECEIVED ANYTHING FROM RICHARD HANSEN'S ESTATE OR TRUST. HOWEVER, TO DATE JOHN HAS RECEIVED:

a. JOHN LIVED RENT FREE, BILL FREE, AND MAINTENANCE FREE FOR MANY MONTHS IN RICHARD HANSEN'S HOME (AFTER HIS DEATH) AT THE EXPENSE OF THE ESTATE. VIOLET HANSEN PAID ALL EXPENSES INCLUDING JOHN'S PERSONAL DEBTS...

b. JOHN WAS GIVEN A CHECK FOR $1000 A LUMP SUM OF CASH OF $450 AND HE WAS FREQUENTLY GIVEN $50 HERE AND $50 THERE.

c. THEN AFTER THE MANNER OF HOW RICHARD HANSEN'S PROPERTY WAS TO BE DISTRIBUTED WAS AGREED UPON, JOHN BEGAN STEALING ITEMS FROM THE ESTATE, INCLUDING

FURNITURE VALUED AT WELL
OVER $2000 AND MANY OTHER
ITEMS.

IN CONCLUSION THERE WAS A
TOTAL OF $101,000 TO BE DISTRIBUTED
AMONG 7 HEIRS. VIOLET HANSEN WAS
REIMBURSED APPROXIMATELY $20,000.
LEAVING APPROX. $80,000 / 7 = $11,428 PER
HEIR.
JOHN HAS RECEIVED IN CASH OR
EQUIVELANT VALUE $6,745. HAD JOHN'S
CONDUCT BEEN TOLERABLE HE WOULD
PERHAPS BE ENTITLED TO $4,683.
JOHN FREQUENTLY CALLS VIOLET
HANSEN (WHILE DRUNK) HARASSING
HER AND OTHER MEMBERS OF THE
FAMILY.
VIOLET HANSEN IS IN POOR
HEALTH AND UNDER A DOCTORS CARE.
IN ORDER TO STOP JOHN'S
HARASSMENT AND BECAUSE HE IS A FAMILY
MEMBER WE OFFER HIM $1,000 ONLY IF HE
SIGNS A DOCUMENT STATING HE WILL NO
LONGER PURSUE THIS MATTER OR HARASS
US.
PLEASE CONTACT DAVID HANSEN IF
YOU HAVE ANYTHING TO DISCUSS.
SINCERELY,
THE HANSEN FAMILY

* * *

The letter from David was one of three sent to Johnny's attorney by the co-beneficiaries of the R.R.H. Trust. He received several phone calls from them as well. Presumably, they were all speaking on Violet's behalf, all giving their opinions as to why Johnny should be excluded from the Trust. The phone calls and letters all followed in the months after the attorney sent the first letter stating his demands to Violet.

Johnny was unable to put credence to his family's behavior. Nothing happened within the family to cause such strife between them and Johnny. He felt that their behavior could only be motivated by pure greed. The letter his brother wrote was almost laughable. In fact, it was somewhat contradictory. What expenses was he talking about? If Nanny paid out twenty thousand dollars, what did she do with it? Why was his dad's estate allowed to go bankrupt if she paid out so much? The few thousand dollars she may have given him didn't cause it. As far as free rent goes, it was his home as well. Patricia stayed living at the house long after Johnny had moved out and in with Kim. No one informed him that he should be paying rent, or to whom he should be paying it. Maybe if someone would have been honest and given him his share of the Trust, he could have paid rent, and Nanny wouldn't have had to slip him a fifty here and there.

Johnny certainly hadn't given Nanny permission to sign his name on anything. Besides, what authority would allow her to do that just because she said she had Johnny's permission? His brother admitted that Johnny was an equal heir to the Trust but believed he was behaving badly. Therefore, the other beneficiaries thought he was entitled to far less than his dad's will stated? Did he really think that he and the others could sway Johnny's attorney into seeing that Johnny's conduct had been less than tolerable, thereby revoking his share of the Trust?

The reference to the codicil of the will was most likely a last-minute attempt to try to exclude Johnny. However, the codicil was null and void, because it was not witnessed and notarized. It stated if any of the heirs were on any type of drugs, the Trustee was to withhold all funds from any of his children until the Trustee was convinced they would not use the money for drugs. Johnny wondered what time frame it pertained to. At any given time, any of his siblings could be on drugs. Their dad made it as much a part of their lives as he did his own.

The attorney, growing weary after making several demands for information and not receiving a reasonable response, wrote Violet a final letter. In it he stated that all the statements and opinions about the Trust and why Johnny should be excluded meant nothing to him or the courts. He reiterated that as Trustee of the Trust, it was Violet's responsibility to preserve and protect the assets of the Trust, and to prevent such waste of the assets. She was also required to fairly administer the Trust for the benefit of all the beneficiaries, including

Johnny Hansen. The attorney allowed her seven days to comply with the law, and suggested that she consult with an attorney to settle with Johnny.

The letter must have gotten Violet's attention, because soon after Johnny's attorney received a letter from her attorney. The letter stated that Violet had decided to get the Trust matters settled once and for all. She, therefore, offered $3,500 to settle all claims with Johnny. The money would come from her personally, and she would have to borrow it. She wanted to avoid any dispute with her grandson, and she wanted to make sure there were no hard feelings in the family.

Johnny mulled over his grandmother's proposition for a few days. He thought her benevolence was almost heartwarming. Did she really think he should accept her meager offer graciously and go on as if nothing happened? He knew that he could drag it out in the courts and eventually win. She may even face prosecution for her unethical behavior as Trustee. After all, she more or less admitted that she depleted Johnny's share of the Trust; why else would she have to borrow the money to pay him?

He decided to settle for the $3,500, although it still bothered him about the money. What the hell did they do with it all? There was no way that the bankruptcy court accounted for everything his father owned. Johnny did find out that the court case his dad brought against Victor Lederman in 1985, and Victor appealed, had finally been settled. Victor lost his appeal, so that was another fifty-plus thousand to the bankruptcy court.

Johnny would find out years later that his father set up a Trust and a signer on the Trust was Richard Machiavelli (a/k/a Richard Hansen). Maybe his father had a plan. His business was suffering so he hid most of his assets in the Trust under his alias, knowing that one day he would be forced to file bankruptcy.

THIRTY-FIVE

In March of 1989, Jill discovered she was pregnant. They were both excited at the prospect of being parents to two children. Mark was especially thrilled about it and used the excuse to go out and celebrate nearly every night. Jill would stay at home with Travis and mark the days until the baby was due.

They welcomed another son into the world that December and named him Gavin Lee St. George. He was delivered by caesarian section, so Jill's stay in the hospital was longer than she expected. Mark was supposedly home caring for Travis. Jill spoke with Johnny on the phone Christmas Eve, and he said that indeed Mark and Travis had been there earlier that evening and had dinner with them, along with the rest of their mom's side of the family and a few of Kim's family members and friends.

The next day Mark picked up Jill and Gavin to take them home. When they arrived, Mark surprised Jill with a rocking chair. She sat down and introduced Travis to his little brother, and watched as Mark put the chair together. Then he announced that he wanted to take a break. He would take a minute to go to the pharmacy and pick up Jill's pain prescription and finish the chair when he got home. Jill had asked him to stop and get it on their way home from the hospital, but he told her he would get it later. Mark was gone for over three days. When he finally returned, he said he had been celebrating the birth of his son. Jill had heard so many excuses that she didn't even know how to respond to him.

Jill numbed herself to the situation with Mark. For the last few years the love she once felt for him, the love that made her feel warm inside, was now making her cold. Each day the resentment she felt for him was growing. She bided her time until she had the courage to walk away.

That day wasn't far off. Not much later, she happened to catch Mark shooting up cocaine. Jill had confronted him in the past about it, once when she had actually found spoons in her car. She wondered why the hell he had them in there. Although she could guess, she also knew that whenever she accused Mark of any wrongdoing, he always had some excuse. And she, trying to avoid confrontation at any cost, would let him off the hook. Not today, though. The needle and spoon he was holding were evidence enough that he was never going to change.

She packed up what she could fit in her car, got the boys, and she left. After driving around for a while she decided to go to her cousin Brenda's. Brenda was single and she welcomed Jill and her boys to stay with her. She was a big help to Jill then, and would be again in the many rough times that followed.

Jill divorced Mark in 1991. Soon after she met a man she considered a blessing. She married Bruce Smith on July 3, 1993. Her boys, Travis and Gavin, grew to love Bruce and called him Dad. Their biological father seemed to have disappeared. There wasn't even as much as a phone call from him in years.

Jill and Bruce wanted to have another baby. Jill became pregnant, and Kelsi Janay Smith was born. Kelsi was a joy, but her delightful presence did nothing to quell the problems that were developing for Jill. She and Bruce couldn't resolve their issues and divorced two years later.

Gradually, the everyday emotional stress of living with her emotional scars started to wear on her. The memories from her childhood started to creep into her thoughts more and more, and each time, they stayed longer. She kept remembering the words Richard once spoke to her. "I'll haunt you forever, even when I'm dead." Everything was becoming confusing to her, and she was losing ground fast. She attempted suicide several times by overdosing on her prescription drugs, and at the last minute, would call her sister.

At this point, she still hadn't talked to anyone about Richard or what he had done to her. Her family was becoming more and more angry with her. They couldn't understand why she couldn't get a grip and pull herself together. She was an intelligent, young, beautiful woman with three great kids. She had everything to live for, didn't she?

Still, Jaqueline kept getting the calls to go to Jill's. Kim and Johnny, and the rest of the family would help out by taking her boys on weekends. Finally, it all came to a head one day when Jaqueline answered the phone and it was ten-year-old Gavin. He begged Jaqueline to please come over and said, "My mom is sleeping on the couch, and she won't wake up."

Jaqueline, being a firefighter and EMT, rushed over to find Jill unconscious. The place was a mess. There was no food in the cupboards, and prescription bottles were all over.

Jill was checked into the psychiatric ward at the hospital. Jaqueline notified everyone, and when Kim and Johnny showed up, Johnny couldn't help crying. The doctors had Jill on eleven different medications, and she was practically incoherent. All anyone could make out of what she was saying was that Richard had raped her.

It was decided that Jill would remain in the mental institution for further evaluation while being weaned off of most of the medications. During her stay at the institute, it came to light how Richard had molested and abused her. Up to this point, the only one who knew was Jaqueline, who had also been molested by him. They had never openly talked about it to each other.

When Jill was released from the institution, she moved in with Kim and Johnny. Kelsi was living with Bruce, and Brenda took in Travis and Gavin. The memories of Richard raping her continued to haunt Jill. She was once again hospitalized.

Her life was filled with sickness and distress over the course of the next ten years. She was hospitalized several more times from suicide attempts, and participated in hours of therapy sessions. On several occasions, she underwent shock therapy in hopes of erasing the memories of Richard molesting her. Sometimes she would sit for hours and write pages upon pages of stories about Richard and what he did to her. Then after years of writing she thought that if she got rid of them all, burned them all up, her memories of him would disappear.

Nothing seemed to work, and to this day, her memories of those horrible years still live with her. She tries to keep them buried deep and far away. If she allows them to seep into her thoughts, she risks having an emotional breakdown. Richard had said he would haunt her from the grave, and he has.

THIRTY-SIX

Johnny felt that the only family members he had left were his sisters, Jill and Jaqueline. There had been no contact between him and anyone on his dad's side of the family for a few years. But during that time he did receive a call from Patricia. He wasn't surprised to hear from her because they had always been close while growing up. She had called Johnny to tell him that Nanny was in hospice care and didn't have long to live. Johnny and Kim went to visit, and Nanny died a few days later.

Although Johnny still harbored feelings of animosity toward his siblings, his need to love and to be loved was stronger. He went on to forgive Niles, David, Linda, Kathy and Patricia, but he would never forget how they treated him. He also decided to overlook what his Grandpa and Grandma Bloom and his Auntie Helen and Uncle Ted thought about his dad. He missed them and the family gatherings they had in the past. He and Kim started spending more time with all of them, taking turns going to each other's homes. They would get together to celebrate Hanukah, Christmas, Thanksgiving, anniversaries, birthdays, and family picnics in the park. Helen and Ted would often invite Johnny and Kim as their guests to join them, along with the rest of Janyce's family, at The Green Gables Country Club, an exclusive Jewish club on the lake. In short, they did their best to be a family.

Kim, who also grew up in a family that celebrated birthdays and holidays together, wanted to keep that tradition alive. She and John hosted several parties over the years, always extending an invitation to anyone in the family who wanted to attend. Most often someone would decline, afraid of running into someone from the other side.

One year Kim and Johnny hosted an elaborate Christmas Eve party. More than sixty guests attended. Among them were David, Kathy, and Patricia. Although Johnny may have forgiven his siblings, Jaqueline couldn't stand them. She was assured beforehand that none of Johnny's "other" family would be there, or else she wouldn't show up. Johnny didn't think they were coming because they hadn't confirmed their invitations.

Jaqueline arrived and went upstairs to put her coat away. When she came back downstairs, she saw David, and immediately ran back to get her coat. She came down the stairs as fast as she could and bolted out of the house before anyone could say anything.

The rest of the evening was a little tense. David sat next to Grandma Bloom, and the two chatted for some time. If Molly realized that she was talking to Richard's son, she didn't let on.

* * *

John was still having a difficult time dealing with the loss of both of his parents and went through a few rough years battling a drinking problem. He would often drink to excess, which put stress on his marriage to Kim. To add to the stress, medical bills started piling up, caused by Kim's medical condition. She was quickly becoming weaker and weaker. After numerous tests, a team of doctors concluded she had a hole in her heart the size of a silver dollar, and other congenital heart defects.

In July 1994, she underwent major open heart surgery. At the time, she was working as a licensed real estate agent, but after her surgery, she was unable to work for months. Everything that Johnny and Kim had been through the last few years put a terrible strain on their marriage. It didn't help matters that they both wanted children, and Kim had a miscarriage. They came close to divorcing, but the love they had for each other won out, and they were determined to turn things around. If they wanted their marriage to work, they both knew the first issue they had to resolve was Johnny's drinking, and on July 13, 1997, he quit.

The following year, Johnny and Kim decided to apply to be foster parents with the intent of one day adopting a child. The county approved their application and immediately placed a handsome five-year-old blond-haired, blue-eyed boy with them. Kim and Johnny were overwhelmed with joy. No one told them that he was known to be the worst child in their county's foster care system and that no other foster homes would take him.

They both tried their best, and the three of them got along great, but it was becoming obvious the placement wasn't going to last. Although it had to be the best six months that little boy had in awhile, Kim and Johnny couldn't deal with the everyday issues. He had been kicked out of daycare, public schools, private bus transportation to his special schooling, and he wasn't even allowed to stay with a babysitter. Sadly, Kim and Johnny made the call to their case worker to tell her they would not be able to adopt him. They worked with the county to have the little boy transitioned and placed with his grandparents, who eventually did adopt him.

Two other children came and went. Heartbroken, Kim and Johnny didn't want the anguish of losing another child, so they gave up on fostering children with the intent to adopt. Several months later, they decided to try again, but this time they would put all their efforts into straight adoption where parental rights had already been relinquished.

Nearly a year went by. It was Christmas time. They saw a picture of a brother and sister on the Adoption Exchange. The girl was six years old and the boy had just turned four. Kim and Johnny applied to adopt them, but were told not to hold their breath because seventy other couples had applied as soon as their pictures appeared on the site.

Three months later, they received a call from the case worker asking if they were still interested in adopting the two. Of course they were. After all of the terrible experiences Johnny had endured, he still managed to come out on top. In January of 2003, he had just celebrated five and a half years of sobriety. Now with a boy and girl, their family was finally complete. The loving father of two beautiful children, Johnny swore that he would practice and instill in his kids only the good qualities that he gleaned from his mother and father.

In spring of 2004, an exciting job opportunity arose, and the family decided to move away from Denver. He, Kim, and their two children now live in Arizona. They see family members whenever possible. Auntie Helen and Uncle Ted still own their home in Denver but spend the winters in Arizona. Johnny's cousin, Brenda, and her family sold their home in Denver and moved to Arizona as well. In November 2008, Auntie Helen moved Grandma Bloom from Denver to a retirement home in Scottsdale, not far from Johnny.

He often talks on the phone with Patricia and David, who still live in Denver. Of course, he is still close to his sisters, Jaqueline and Jill.

THIRTY-SEVEN

John, Kim, and their two children were returning home after spending an enjoyable afternoon visiting their Grandma Bloom and celebrating her 100th birthday. Grandma Bloom had aged well. Although it had been a few years since she reiterated the phrase, "That bastard killed our Janny," the loss of her daughter was every bit as painful for her as it had been twenty-five years ago. Yet, her memories of Janny were every bit as beautiful.

Up until a little over a year before, Grandma Bloom had resided in her own home in Denver—the same home where she lived with her husband, Ben, for more than forty-two years. Since Grandpa Bloom's passing, nearly fourteen years before, Grandma had lived in the house alone with the exception of the last few years when Jill moved in to help out with the everyday chores.

Although Grandma got around fairly well, Helen had decided to move her into the retirement home in Scottsdale, Arizona, so she wouldn't have to travel back and forth to Denver from Scottsdale all the time to see her mother. At first, Grandma wasn't at all happy that Helen had uprooted her from the only home she had known for more than fifty-five years. Each time Johnny and his family would visit Grandma at the retirement home, she would ask, "When will I get to go home, Johnny? I want to go home." She finally settled in and was happy with her new friends and frequent family visits.

When she moved to Arizona, Jill continued living at her house.

After Johnny and his family returned home from the birthday celebration, Jill joined them. Although she just saw them at the party, she could hardly wait to spend time with them. The last time she saw them was a brief visit a couple years ago.

When the doorbell rang, the whole family hurried to the door, including Zak, their twelve-year-old Blue Sable German Sheppard. Although it had only been a few hours since they had seen each other, they were all hugging as if it had been years.

Zak remembered Jill and not wanting to be left out, jumped up and started licking her face. Everyone laughed, and a few happy, emotional tears were shed.

"What a beautiful house you have," Jill said.

"Thanks," Kim replied. "Come on in. I'll show you around while Johnny takes your bags to your room."

Jill glanced through the windows in the back of the house and said, "You're so lucky to have your own pool. I would love to go swimming. I wish Grandma's house had a pool."

"It is still a little chilly." Kim took her arm. "But if it warms up, we'll go."

"That sounds perfect," Jill said. "I'm looking forward to sitting down with you and John. I have a lot on my mind I need to talk about."

After showing Jill the rest of the house, Kim left her in her room to get settled while she went to make some iced tea. After making the tea she went to get Jill. As she approached her room, she overheard her talking to Elizabeth*, Kim and Johnny's adopted daughter.

"Don't ever, ever hold things inside," Jill told Elizabeth. "If you have a problem, if someone does something to you that you don't want them to do, tell someone. Even if that person said they would hurt you if you tell, just tell. It will be okay."

Kim entered the room and said, "The tea is ready. Do you want to sit down in the family room and talk?"

"Yes, Kimmy," Jill replied. "I think I need to. There's a lot I have to say."

From the conversation she just overheard, Kim wasn't quite sure what Jill wanted to talk about, but thought it might have to do with Richard. Sensing where their conversation might lead, Kim sent the children into the movie room to watch television.

Kim served iced tea and passed a tray of appetizers, as the three of them sat down in the family room—Johnny and Kim on the leather couch and Jill next to them in an oversized comfy chair.

Jill spoke first. "You know, Johnny, I'm really sorry about how badly I treated you when we were growing up."

"What do you mean Jill? He asked. "We were just kids. Don't worry about it."

"But I was so mean to you at times. I feel guilty. Now, I think that maybe I was just taking my anger out on you, because of how Richard treated us. Richard treated you bad enough. You sure didn't need me bullying you around too."

"If you feel you were mean to me, I forgive you," Johnny told her. "As I said, we were just kids. As far as my dad goes, I've dealt with the anger and hate I had toward him. I don't agree with his actions, but I've accepted the fact that they were just his way. The last few months before Dad died, we actually got along well and formed a good father and son relationship. You have to admit he wasn't all bad. He did a lot with us. Look at all the family things we did together, like all the vacations we went on and everything he taught us."

"Are you kidding me?" Jill started to cry, and her voice was getting louder as she spoke. "Were you frickin blind? You guys might have been having fun, but you didn't notice what the bastard was doing to me. All those fun vacations and everything he was teaching us? What a frickin joke. Every chance he got, he did something disgusting to me, and it wasn't just in my bed. He did things like stick his finger up me when he was putting me on a horse, and pulling my swimming suit down and feeling me up when he was teaching me how to swim. You don't know the half of what so-called Daddy Dicky did to me."

Johnny was stunned. "I'm so sorry," he said. "I wasn't aware that he was doing those things to you."

"You don't have to be sorry. There was nothing you could have done. If Mom couldn't have done anything to stop it, then you sure couldn't have."

"Did Mom know?" Johnny asked.

"I never told her, if that's what you mean, but she must have been aware about some of it."

Kim got up and handed Jill a tissue. "Here, Jill. You don't have to do this to yourself right now. We can talk again later."

"Oh no," Jill said. "I'm fine. I have held all this in for way too long. Besides, I don't really want to talk anymore about myself. I want to talk about Mom. Johnny, there are a few things you need to know. After I tell you, then you might not think so kindly of your dad."

"Look, Jill. I know how bad he treated Mom, but don't you think that she could have left him if she really wanted to? She must have stayed because she loved him. Look at everything he did for her. She had all the money she could ever want, a new house, new car, designer clothes, and vacations. The only time I ever saw them fight is when Dad was drunk."

Johnny fell silent for a moment. He didn't like feeling the need to defend his dad to Jill. She could hate him all she wanted to, Johnny thought, but for God's sake, the man was dead. Why couldn't she just leave it alone? Johnny knew why. He had lived in the same hell with all of them, and he too thought about the past on a regular basis. The difference between him and Jill was that he came to terms with his past and dealt with it, and Jill couldn't.

"Maybe Mom did love Richard," Jill said, "but she hated him too, and she wanted to leave him so many times. You know that as well as I do. He threatened to kill her if she did leave. A lot went on between Richard and Mom while you were in college and away in the service. Even though I wasn't living at home most of the time, I talked to Mom a lot about it, and what she didn't tell me, Nancy did. I think he did finally end up killing her."

Johnny closed his eyes and thought for a moment. *Oh boy, here we go again. The same old crap that everyone was saying twenty-five years ago. Richard killed Janyce.*

"There's no sense dredging up all that again. You know, Jill, you're just like the rest of them. They all want to blame my dad for killing Mom, but what the hell are they basing it on? Do you know something about that night that I don't?"

Jill answered with a quiet voice. "Maybe I know a little more about that night than you do, but that's not what I'm talking about. I'm talking about the night around Thanksgiving a few months before she died. Richard beat her up so badly at the hotel where they were staying that she ended up in the emergency room. She was black and blue from head to toe. He beat her over and over again with the heel of his boot and broke her arm. She had sixty-eight stitches in her head. She did manage to leave him then. She was here in Arizona for a few weeks staying with Auntie Helen and Uncle Ted. Even then he wouldn't leave her alone. He hounded the hell out of her until she made the choice to go back to him."

Holding back tears, Johnny finally spoke, his voice shaking. "Why didn't anyone tell me? How could I have not known about this?"

"Mom didn't want anyone else to know, especially us kids," Jill said. "I found out about it from Nancy, because she was at home the night it happened. A few days later, I flew down here to see Mom. God, Johnny. It was so sad. She was all bruised. You couldn't even see an inch of normal-colored flesh on her. She had a broken arm and stitches all over her head."

Tears streamed down his face. "It's hard to think about everything that Mom had to go through in her short life. She literally went through hell, and I didn't do a damn thing to help her. And now she's dead. What kind of a son was I?"

"You were only a kid," Jill said. "What could you do? No one else could help her. Not even Grandma and Grandpa. Richard was a very powerful man and had connections in high places."

"You know this might sound a little crass right now, and I'm not trying to stick up for my dad, but none of this means that he killed her."

The three sat in silence for a few minutes wiping away tears. Then trying to lighten the mood a little, Johnny said, "You know what? We should write a book. But who would believe it? Kim and I have talked about it before. At one point, I even tried writing a few pages."

Jill laughed. "That's funny, because I wrote several hundred pages over the span of a few years, and I ended up throwing them all away."

"Maybe we should really get serious about this," Kim said. "I can ask my sister, Sherrie, if she would be willing to write the book for us."

The rest of the evening was spent with the three reminiscing about the past. Jill and Johnny shared many memories with each other that night, some either had forgotten and some never known.

THIRTY-EIGHT

When Jill returned to Denver, she was eager to start on the book. It would be easier to accomplish now that she had found out that Johnny shared the same interest in writing their story. She thought to herself, it's funny how you can communicate with someone for years, but never really talk. It seems that's what had happened between her and Johnny.

Now, she was so happy to have had the chance to sit down with her brother and really talk. It did her a world of good to get things out in the open. She was surprised how easy the words came to her. Once she started talking, it was as if she couldn't stop. She shared memories with Johnny and Kim that she had never told anyone before. Johnny had to have felt the same way when recounting the past. A lot of things she suspected he had never told anyone before either. Jill could tell by the way Kim gasped a few times that she was hearing some of Johnny's stories for the first time.

Jill was ready to do her part for the book. Her plan was to record everything she could remember and then send the disks to Kim. The bad memories would come easy. They were the kind that cut so deep into her soul, a constant irritation, even when she wasn't thinking of them. Although the memories would come easily, they would hurt, so she had been mentally preparing herself for this. She didn't want to risk having another breakdown.

Jill prepared herself a hot cup of tea and sat down in her favorite chair to start recording. It was the chair her grandma always sat in. Jill missed her grandma. The house was so quiet, and she felt so alone with her gone. Sometimes just sitting in the chair made her feel better.

As she progressed through the years, each session was getting harder for her to get through. At times, she would burst into tears and have no choice but to stop recording. Trying everything and anything to deal with the pain, Jill started self-medicating, until getting to the point where she had taken too much. She realized something was wrong and called her son Gavin. He rushed over and took her to the emergency room. Her kidneys were failing, so she was admitted to the hospital. She stayed there for a few days until her kidneys were functioning normally, and she was back on track with her medication.

She returned home alone after her stay at the hospital eager to continue with her recordings. There were only a few more to get through. Jill had her mind set on seeing this book through to the end. She made a silent vow to herself that she would not allow Richard to interfere again. The bastard had already stripped her of ever feeling a shred of dignity or respect for herself. She'd be damned if she would allow him to take her life too. She would live to tell the whole world about the son-of-a-bitch and everything he had done to her and her mother.

Still, it became more difficult for her to talk about her memories, and each word was becoming harder to speak. She could feel herself slowly slipping away into the dark place. It was her very own place where she went to be alone, and no one was allowed to enter. She stopped recording and sent the disk to Kim on Thursday, June 4, 2009.

The next day, Friday, June 5, 2009, Jill was hospitalized again. On Saturday, June 6, 2009, she fell into a coma, and her kidneys and liver were failing. The doctors, fearing the worst, told the family to be prepared as she most likely would not recover this time. Her two sons and sister were notified, and they hurried to the hospital. Jill's daughter was away on a cruise and couldn't be reached until later.

Her nurse called Johnny at his home to give him the bad news. He had a flight to Denver scheduled for the next morning for training for his job, and he would be staying in a hotel near the training facility. Jill had planned to pick him up from the airport.

He and Kim cried most of the day. They couldn't help but feel that they were partly to blame for Jill's breakdown. They had realized in the beginning that it wasn't going to be easy for her, and they feared she wasn't emotionally stable enough to begin working on the book, but Jill had insisted. They should have put a stop to it after listening to the first tapes. If she ended up dying, they would blame themselves for not trying to dissuade her into waiting.

When Johnny arrived in Denver, Jaqueline was at the airport waiting to pick him up. They drove to the hospital where they met with the rest of the family. As they gathered by Jill's bedside, they held out little hope that she could ever recover. She had already been through so much and managed to survive, but this seemed to be the worst. As the hours passed and everyone waited, Jill seemed to be getting better. Miraculously, to everyone's disbelief, she came out of her coma.

Several times during the writing of this book, she would have a near breakdown or succumb to an illness, only to be pulled back from the brink of sometimes certain death. For a while, she was in and out of the hospital on a weekly basis. She ended up back in the psych ward and elected to undergo electro shock therapy again in the hopes of erasing her memories of Richard. She was there for six weeks before going home.

Jill was released the day before Thanksgiving 2009. It also happened to be her forty-ninth birthday. Gavin picked her up and took her home to where a very special homecoming awaited her. Jaqueline, along with Travis and Gavin, had cleaned the house spotless. Before Jill got home, they went shopping and stocked her cupboards and refrigerator full of food. They purchased a turkey and all the trimmings for a Thanksgiving dinner, which Jill and her kids celebrated together the next day. Jill was overcome with emotion. Thanks to her kids and Jaqueline, she was the happiest she had been in months.

Kim could almost hear the life literally being sucked out of Jill as she listened to the recordings. One particular disk, Jill began screaming, as if Richard were in the room with her, "You f***er, you f***er, you f***er. You killed my mother." Johnny had finished recording a few tapes, so Kim started to transcribe them. It was much easier for her to listen to his recordings. Although she found herself crying for the helpless little boy more than once, she didn't feel the way she had when she listened to Jill's disks. Kim was even able to laugh at some of Johnny's stories as he told them. She could definitely sense the hatred and anger that came across as Jill spoke. When listening to her husband speak, she sensed that he didn't harbor the feelings that Jill did. Kim was proud that he was able to sort out his feelings and move on.

THIRTY-NINE

Although Johnny and Jill had provided plenty of information about their lives, some things needed to be verified. First, Kim wanted to focus on trying to get as many details as she could about the night Janyce died. They felt the police report would be an essential piece of information, but Jill had long since lost her copy. Kim was doubtful anything could be obtained now, given how Jill was told twenty-five years ago by the police to forget about it. Either way, they had to try.

Kim got busy on the internet looking for anything that remotely related to Richard or Janyce. Meanwhile, Sherrie placed a call to the Aurora Police Department. Eventually, she was able to speak to Detective Steve Conner with the Cold Case/Major Homicide Unit. She explained to him that she was trying to obtain as much information as she could for a book she was writing. He was very helpful. Detective Conner found the file and relayed to Sherrie the case number for future reference. He said that there was a handwritten note attached to the report, presumably written by the chief of police in 1984. The note stated that the complete police report could be released, but the polygraph tests could not. Detective Conner said that given the case was twenty-five years old, he saw no reason why they couldn't be released now. He would have everything sent to Johnny's home address. The Aurora Police Department didn't have computers at that time, so all the reports had to be scanned and entered into their records system. Given the volume of current work they had, it could take up to several weeks before anything was sent out.

With a case number in hand, a call was then made to obtain the photos taken of the crime scene that early morning in 1984. To their total disbelief, with Detective Conner's permission, APD agreed to release all twenty-one CSI photos to Johnny. They couldn't believe their luck. They had no expectations of ever obtaining the police report, let alone the polygraph test. Now they were also getting the photos, as well. They were well on their way to having everything necessary to write the book.

Sherrie then made a call to the Arapahoe County Coroner's Office. They agreed to e-mail the contents of the file they had on Janyce.

In June of 2009, Kim walked down to the end of the block to get the mail. A large manila envelope with a return address for the Aurora Police Department was in their mailbox. Barely able to contain her excitement, she ran home and burst into the house calling, "Johnny, Johnny, guess what I have?"

He assumed that the envelope contained the police report. Excited, yet filled with apprehension, he said, "I don't think I can touch it even. You'll have to read it to me. "

Sitting down, Kim read through the entire report, stopping from time to time only to see the effect it was having on Johnny. There were several pages, with each officer on the scene that early morning submitting their own handwritten or typed narrative. As Johnny listened, he was confronted with an array of emotions. Kim continued to read as he expressed shock, sadness, anger, and frustration. She finished reading over the police reports and the polygraphs. It was a lot to take in, but Johnny got the gist of it.

"Do you realize what the hell you just read?" he said to Kim. "My mom didn't commit suicide. It was an accident. Dad and Mom were both drinking. They started fighting, and then it turned violent just like a million times before. The only difference is this time it got out of hand. Dad accidentally killed her, and then tried to cover it up. You know, Kim, Grandma and Grandpa Bloom, Auntie Helen, and the rest weren't so far off from the truth when they said that Dad killed my mom. But they think it was intentional, and knowing how Dad and Mom were, I know that it was an accident. I am so mad and disgusted with Jaqueline right now. Why was she so willing to believe that Mom killed herself? Then she wanted me to believe it too, and I did. It makes me sick thinking about it. I disgraced Mom's memory all these years for even believing that shit. Especially for Jaqueline not to even try to find out what really happened. She just accepted it. *Oh, Mom committed suicide. Just let it go, Johnny.* What the hell did I do about it, Kim? Not a damn thing. I could have tried to at least get a police report or something. But no, I did absolutely nothing."

"You were in the service," she said. "Besides, just look at what you're doing now. Now is what's important. You're finding out the truth, and you're honoring your mom's memory by writing this book."

* * *

The photos arrived several days later. Johnny was at work, so Kim waited to tell him when he arrived home. They had decided that she wouldn't call him at work anymore to discuss the book. Johnny arrived home, and Kim and the kids greeted him at the door, as usual. Kim followed Johnny back to the master bedroom, and said, "The pictures came today."

"Did they?" he said. "Let me change out of this suit, and then I'll look at them."

Now that they were actually there, he was afraid. He wondered what all the pictures were of and knew that some would be of his mom, and she would be dead. He didn't want to see her that way. He wanted to keep the last memory he had of her waving at him and smiling while the sun shone down on her beautiful face.

He walked out of the bedroom.

"Kim, I can't look at the pictures, but tell me what each of them is."

Kim had never met Janny, and she was afraid to look at the photos but she began to describe each one to Johnny. One in particular made her gasp and begin to tear up. It was a picture of his mother, dead, lying on her back on the floor with her eyes open.

Seeing Kim's reaction, Johnny said, "Just show me the pictures of the cars and purses. I can't look at any of my mom." He skimmed through them and said he wanted to wait to look at them in detail.

* * *

It was Saturday morning a week later. Kim and Johnny were sitting outside by the pool having morning coffee. Johnny asked Kim, "Will you go get the pictures? I want to look at them."

"Are you sure?"

He nodded. "That's all I've been thinking about all week. I can sit here and badmouth Jaqueline for not even trying to obtain a police report, and here I am. I'm sitting here with crime scene photos of what happened right in front of me, and I didn't even bother to look at them."

Kim knew that eventually Johnny would want to see them, so she had prearranged them in order so that the one of his mom with her eyes open was the last one he would look at.

Johnny held the pictures in his hands. One by one he looked slowly at each one, as if mentally trying to bring life to it. The cars in the garage. His mom's passenger door open. Her shoe on the garage floor, with a red hand towel lying nearby. Johnny had a mental image of his dad crying and screaming as he pulled her from the car.

The next was a picture of his mom's purse on the bathroom vanity. A slight smile formed on his mouth as he thought of how tidy and organized she was. Her purse even showed it. The next picture was of his mom lying on the floor, her body covered with a white sheet that wasn't quite big enough. Her feet and hands were extended out from under the sheet, and at the top, he could see her dark brown tousled hair.

Johnny's breathing quickened, as he slowly brought up the last picture. His mother was lying on her back on the carpeted floor. Her eyes were open, and she had a black, four-string beaded choker necklace around her neck. She was wearing a lavender dress that was cut open from the waist up. Her breasts were exposed for the purpose of performing resuscitation.

"God, Kim," he said. "She looks like she's fake, like a dummy. It's so surreal, as if I'm looking at crime scene pictures from a movie, not my own mom."

Johnny gently laid the pictures down. He closed his eyes and sat back in the chair and cried.

* * *

The eighteen-page police report and three polygraph tests stayed on the coffee table within arm's reach. Johnny spent hours reading over each page. He was trying to make sense of what really happened to his mom. It seemed the more he read, the more questions he had. A knot formed in his stomach. He started getting that sick feeling as he had so many times before. Like when his dad was about to punish him or starting to knock his mom around. He shared his thoughts with Kim.

She had been reading over the reports, as well, and was forming her own opinions as to what really happened to Janyce.

"Come here," she told him. "I want to show you something."

Johnny followed her into their home office. She sat down at the computer desk.

"You know," she told him, "none of this is making any sense. There are so many things in the reports and polygraphs that raise red flags. For one thing, the coroner's preliminary report stated that your mom was wearing a black beaded necklace and that it broke when they tried to resuscitate her. We both wondered why it was on her neck for the pictures. When I scanned them to the computer, I zoomed in on them. Look at this and tell me what you think."

Kim had the picture on the screen zoomed in, showing only Janyce's neck with the necklace on.

"Do you see what I see?" she asked.

"It looks like there are welts and red marks on her neck," he said.

"And look at this area on her ribcage under her right breast. It looks like a large bruise. It also looks as if she was struck on the left side of her face near her hairline. And if you look at the picture closely, the one with her eyes open, you can tell she had probably been crying. Her makeup is smeared. It said in the police report the paramedics tried to resuscitate her, but why would they when it was obvious she had been dead for awhile? Her eyes were opened and cloudy, and rigor mortis was already setting in. It just doesn't add up."

"You know," Johnny said, "the more I read over those reports and polygraphs, and now seeing these pictures, I'm starting to hate my dad. I think there's a strong possibility that he really did kill my mom."

FORTY

Johnny and Kim decided that his sister Patricia must have witnessed everything that happened that night. Neighbors were awakened by the noise. She couldn't have slept through it.

"I think she knows the truth and has kept it to herself all these years," Johnny said. "If you really think about it, how could she stay sleeping while Dad was dragging Mom into the house and screaming? The neighbors wake up, but she doesn't? She claims to have slept right up until he made the phone call for help. I think she kind of slipped up when she told Jill that Mom and Dad were arguing that night. Then the police report states that Patricia told Dad he sucks. I bet she doesn't even realize that anyone knows about that."

"I'll bet you're right," she said.

That's it, Kim. I've had it with her. I'm calling her right now, and I'm going to find out what really happened. She wanted me to believe all these years that my mom would actually take her own life, and she knows that she didn't."

"You can't just call her out of the blue and start accusing her of knowing that your dad killed your mom," Kim said. "You'll risk alienating her, and then she won't tell you anything. She has no idea that we're even remotely suspicious of her knowing about anything that happened."

"You're right. We get along well. If I call her up and accuse her of keeping a secret like that, she probably won't ever talk to me again. I'll give it some more thought before I call her."

"The death certificate we have is the amended one," Kim said. "We need to obtain the original one to see why it was amended. Maybe it said suicide on that one."

"So what if it did? That only means that they thought it was suicide, and then they changed it because they didn't know for sure. But if they didn't know for sure, why didn't they do an autopsy? We have to find out what the hell went on back then. You would think a bunch of adolescents were running the coroner's office."

"What if someone was purposely trying to hide something?" Kim asked.

"You might be right. Especially when the coroner says that Mom died from carbon monoxide poisoning, but yet they weren't willing to write suicide as the cause of death on the death certificate. I want that death certificate changed, or else I want a damn good reason why my mom's death was recorded as undetermined."

"First thing in the morning, I'll make a few calls," she told him. "I'll call the coroner's office and find out the differences in the original death certificate and the amended one. Then, maybe, I should contact Detective Conner, the cold case detective who released the police reports to us. I can talk to him about all of our doubts and why he thinks the case was closed so early on. Maybe he would be willing to reopen it."

FORTY-ONE

A phone call led to Vicky Lovato, the lead detective originally assigned to Janyce's case. She still lived in the area and was retired from the Aurora Police Department. Upon talking to her, Sherrie learned that she was the first woman detective on the police force at the Aurora Police Department. Much was left unsaid, but the overtone of the conversation was that, because she was a woman, she was more or less left on her own to work on the case.

When asked specifically about it, she replied that over the years, she worked on a lot of different cases, but this one stuck out in her mind. In fact, when she retired, she took her notes and copies from a few of the case files that she had worked on home with her, and this case was one of them. She said she kept copies of the complete file, along with all her notes, just in case this ever went to trial. She knew somebody was hiding something, but there wasn't enough evidence to bring charges against Richard.

None of us involved with this book ever met with Lovato in person. On the few occasions speaking with her on the phone, she was very forthcoming and candid. In the last phone conversation with her, she agreed to send copies of some of the things she had in her personal file. One item was a copy of the summons that Richard received the night he beat Janyce at the Denver Marriot Hotel SE, the same summons that had the handwritten note on the back threatening the arresting officers. She also had a copy of Richard's mug shot from that night.

Another item was a copy of the letter Richard wrote to Helen saying if he had his way, Janyce would have been buried in a hole head first. Detective Lovato told us that when she was working on this case, she took a copy of these things, along with the crime scene photos, down to the Arapahoe County District Attorney's Office, but no one would help her.

We waited patiently for weeks to get the copies, but never received anything from her. We called, left messages, and Kim has sent her e-mails, which have been opened, but not responded to. Why?

We also placed calls to both Officer Huffman and Lt. Turner. When we asked Turner about that night, he stated that it was a case that stood out in his mind. He also said that there was a lot of confusion as to how Janyce died. They thought that she had a heart attack or committed suicide.

When Officer Huffman was asked about that night, he said that although he had worked on many cases, this one has never left him. He had a feeling something wasn't quite right, and he felt someone was hiding something. When asked if he saw Janyce's body, he said yes. He remembers her sitting in the car, and she was fully clothed. He said that should all be included in his report. Other than Richard, Officer Huffman is the only person who told us he saw Janyce sitting in the car. Kim told him that the copy of his statement we received from the Aurora Police Department doesn't state that anywhere. He asked her to read his report to him. It was just over one page in length. Officer Huffman was surprised there wasn't more. He said maybe he wasn't remembering it right. Kim told him it appeared there may be pages missing from the copy she had. Officer Huffman told her he would pull the case file and look at it.

He also said he knew it was the home of Niles' parents because he had gone to high school with Niles. There is no mention in any of the police reports that Niles was there that night.

Since that phone conversation, we have sent e-mails to Officer Huffman and left messages on his answering machine, but have heard nothing.

When we finally located Karen, the witness who had lived across the street from Richard and Janyce, she was happy to speak with us, but didn't want us to use her real name in the book. She wasn't able to tell us more about that night other than what she had already told the police. She did say that Richard was yelling extremely loud, and that's what woke her. She never heard how Janyce died, and that there seemed to be an air of mystery surrounding her death.

We asked what kind of neighbors the Hansens were. Karen said that she didn't know them on a personal basis, and she hadn't lived there that long. It seemed like the police were watching them though, because there were police cars coming and going on a regular basis at all hours of the day and night, and there were always parties going on. She did notice a lot of young, scantily dressed females coming and going.

Karen went on to tell us that one time a police officer went to the Hansens' door. Richard came out, dressed in a robe, and took off running down the street, and around the corner with the policeman running after him. Karen's son happened to be out riding his bicycle and saw the whole thing. Apparently, around the corner a man was on a roof working and yelled to the police officer "Do you want me to tackle him?" Taking the cue from the officer, the man jumped on Richard and wrestled him to the ground. The officer handcuffed Richard and took him away in the police car. Karen's son came home telling her the story and repeated over and over again, "Mr. Hansen is a pimp. Mr. Hansen is a pimp."

FORTY-TWO

Kim called the Arapahoe County Corner's Office and spoke with the medical investigator, Sarah Saile. The only documents she found in Janyce's file at the coroner's office were the coroner's preliminary report and what seems to be a partial toxicology report. Sarah said that Dr. Woods, who was the coroner in 1984, kept his files at his home. Since he passed away, no one knows where those records are. Sarah went through all the case files that were in the coroner's office during the year 1984—as well as other 1980 case files—just in case Janyce's file had been misfiled. She assured Kim that no other records were found for Janyce.

Kim told Sarah about the pictures she and Johnny received from the crime lab taken the night Janyce died. She said it looked as if Janyce had some bruising on her body and face, as well as welts on her neck. She and Sarah arranged for Kim to scan the photos and police report and e-mail them to the new coroner, Dr. Michael Dobersen, Forensic Pathologist/Coroner/Medical Examiner for Arapahoe County, so he could look at them.

While Kim was waiting for Dr. Dobersen to get back with her about the photographs, she called Cold Case Detective Steven Conner with the Aurora Police Department. Through telephone conversations and e-mails, Kim relayed to him all of the suspicions the family had surrounding Janyce's death, and how they believed it may have been a cover-up. Detective Conner agreed to look into it.

He asked Kim to e-mail to him a list of questions the family had, the names of Richard's closest friends and business associates, along with other details. He told Kim he would look it over and see what he could do, but couldn't promise anything.

* * *

Dr. Dobersen called Kim, and they discussed the photos and police reports. He said that the discoloration under Janyce's right breast did appear to be bruising. By what he could see, the bruising began just under her right breast, and ran all the way down below her stomach area. Its green color indicated that the bruise was probably one to two days old. He said she must have taken a pretty hard blow to that area by a blunt force object, or a hard kick. The reddish color on the left inside corner of her mouth could be dried blood.

They also discussed the black choker necklace wrapped tightly around Janyce's neck (the same one the coroner said was apparently broken during resuscitation efforts), and whether or not the welts and redness could be the result of strangulation. Kim questioned why Janyce's eyes were open, when Richard said he found her unconscious in the car, not to mention the toxicology report stating that Janyce's carbon monoxide level in her system was four times the lethal amount. At the very least, shouldn't she have slipped into a coma (meaning her eyes would be closed) and vomited? Yet, her eyes were open, and there were no signs of vomiting. Strangulation was considered a crime of passion, and the victim's eyes usually remained open. Dr. Dobersen asked Kim if anyone mentioned seeing any hoses in the garage. Kim said not that she knew of, and the police reports certainly didn't state finding any.

They also discussed how Richard could have made it past the open car door without taking the time to close it and then reopen it. In Richard's statement to the police, he said he dragged Janyce out of the Mercedes convertible from the passenger side and into the house. In the photos, the passenger door is open and nearly touching the other Mercedes parked next to it in the garage, and the overhead garage door is closed. The entry into the house from the garage is in front of the car.

Dr. Dobersen went on to tell Kim that he located Janyce's original death certificate. Kim told him that John had a copy of Janyce's amended death certificate and hadn't seen the original one. Since Dr.

Dobersen didn't have a copy of the amended one, Kim scanned and e-mailed a copy to him. In turn, he e-mailed a copy of the original death certificate to her.

The original certificate was never recorded with the registrar; the amended death certificate was recorded on October 30, 1984. Janyce's age was listed as forty-six on the original death certificate, and was changed to forty-five on the amended one. The funeral directors' names were different. Dr. Dobersen explained to Kim that whatever funeral director was available at the time would sign the death certificate.

The most disturbing difference between the two is that her original death certificate states she had an autopsy, but the amended certificate states that no autopsy was performed. Gabriel Goldsmith, Deputy Coroner, signed the original death certificate on September 22, 1984. It should be noted that the coroner's office originally told Detective Lovato if the coroner decided an autopsy would be performed, it would be done on September 22, 1984. The amended death certificate was signed on September 29, 1984 by John M. Wood M.D., coroner, stating there was no autopsy performed.

Kim pointed out to Dr. Dobersen that Janyce's family demanded an autopsy. In addition, in Detective Lovato's original police report, it states that she telephoned the coroner's office on September 25, 1984, expecting to obtain the results of the autopsy. Ken Wilks informed her that one was not performed because the coroner was unavailable, and that no family member requested one. Dr. Dobersen replied that was totally unacceptable. He said if Dr. Wood wasn't available, then someone else would have performed it. Either way, Janyce's body should never have been released from the coroner's office without a full autopsy.

He told Kim he was appalled at the way Dr. Wood handled Janyce's case. The file was missing, other than the few pages he sent to Kim, along with the original death certificate. Dr. Dobersen said there was no question that an autopsy should have been performed. He wished that he had more to go on, and he never liked to see the cause of death go undetermined on a death certificate—and until that was changed, Janyce's case would remain open.

He told Kim that after reviewing the documents, he could not confirm one way or the other if Janyce did or did not have an autopsy.

"This case is exactly why I don't run my office like that," he told her. "Innocent families have to be left with so many doubts and always wondering why."

Dr. Dobersen also brought up the possibility of exhuming Janyce's body, but he would need cooperation from the Aurora Police Department. He told Kim about a recent case he had where a body was exhumed. A fifteen-year old case had been reopened, because the family had their suspicions that the deceased was murdered by her husband. Dr. Dobersen, along with the detective, got a court order and flew to where her body was buried. Her body was exhumed and, although, only bones remained, he was able to prove that she was strangled.

Kim explained to Dr. Dobersen that Janyce had a Jewish burial, which meant her body wasn't embalmed, and she was buried in a simple casket. He said that after twenty-five years, there wouldn't be much of a chance that any of Janyce's remains would be left. He also said that the coroner was the only one who could change a death certificate, but without further evidence, he would not be able to do so.

Kim relayed what she and Dr. Dobersen discussed to Detective Conner through an e-mail. Detective Conner replied telling her that if Dr. Dobersen informed them that a previously reported death had been ruled something other than a homicide, and was now a homicide, then they would assign a detective to investigate. Although Detective Conner agreed that it was possible that Richard killed Janyce, as the family believed, without any evidence, he didn't feel the need to pursue the investigation.

As Kim was busy with her research and phone calls, John got in touch with an investigative reporter who worked for a local newspaper in Denver. John discussed the case with him, and he agreed to see if he could find out anything. The reporter did tell John that if someone wanted to commit a crime in Denver, the seventies and eighties were the best time to do it because they would probably have gotten away with it, and many cases back then went unsolved.

The reporter did a little research and made a few phone calls, but ultimately decided it was in his best interest not to pursue the case or run the story because he didn't have enough proof of anything.

Our next focus was the funeral home, where they must have had a file on Janyce. Was either of the funeral directors who had signed the death certificates around? Did anyone remember the funeral? Was anyone still around who would have prepared Janyce for burial? Her body would have been washed and wrapped in a white shroud, according to Jewish custom. If so, they might remember if she had an autopsy. Could a body be exhumed?

One of the funeral directors told Kim that Rose Hill Cemetery, where Janyce was buried, was among one of the most orthodox cemeteries in the world. He basically told her they would have to move heaven and earth to have her body exhumed from there. So, for the time being, that wasn't an option.

Kim finally spoke with one of the directors at the funeral home who seemed willing to help. Apparently, there was quite a large file that had accumulated on Janyce. He would be happy to share the information with her. Kim told him that the family was looking for any evidence that Janyce had an autopsy. She was also looking for a copy of a certain letter that Richard had sent to several people stating how he wanted Janyce to be buried, head first. He said there was a letter in the file from Richard stating how he wanted Janyce buried, but he had to get permission from the owner of the funeral home before he could release a copy of it.

Later that day, Kim received a call back from the owner himself stating we would need a court order before any of Janyce's file could be released to us, and that no one should have been talking to her about the file.

Kim contacted Dr. Dobersen and relayed to him what the funeral home told her, hoping that he might be able to obtain a copy of Janyce's file without a court order. Dr. Dobersen told Kim since Janyce's family was requesting it, they were entitled to anything the funeral home had in Janyce's file, without a court order.

Kim telephoned the owner of the funeral home again and relayed to him what Dr. Dobersen had told her. This time he agreed to give her the information she was looking for, and he told her there was nothing in the file to indicate Janyce had an autopsy.

Kim requested a copy of the letter they had in their file from Richard be e-mailed to her. The owner scanned the letter and emailed it to Kim while he was still on the phone with her. Although it wasn't the letter they were expecting, it did state the reasons why Richard wasn't going to pay for the funeral. His (unedited) handwritten letter to the

funeral home (received by the funeral home on October 21, 1985
follows—certain names have been changed or omitted):

> *Dear Sirs,*
>
> *My wife's sister Helen is responsible for payment of
> Janyce's funeral.*
>
> *I am a non-practicing Catholic and Janyce was a
> non-practicing Jew. We agreed that we would be buried
> together in a non-partisan cemetery. When Janyce died,
> Helen convicated her body and made all arrangements
> without my knowledge or approval. She refused to allow
> my family to visit Janyce in accordance with our customs.*
>
> *The entire burial was improper. Burying a non-
> practicing Jew in an Orthodox cemetery is an insult to
> the person, the Jewish religion and me personally.*
>
> *The funeral home dealt with Helen in every detail
> without consulting me. This entire matter has upset me
> and added to my personal grief. If I get one more bill or
> notice of this from you or the funeral home, I will file a
> harrasement suit. The money is not an issue with me it
> is the principle.*
>
> *I will spend $20,000.00 to keep from paying this
> bill.*
>
> *The estate does have a stock that can be conveyed
> for payment. Take it or leave it.*
>
> *Richard R. Hansen*

FORTY-THREE

Kim called the veterans' hospital in Denver where Richard died to see if they had any of his medical records, and, if so, what documents were required in order to get them released to John. They were mostly interested in knowing when Richard contracted AIDS, and if by chance, he uttered a deathbed confession. She was told that they did have medical records on Richard, but they were in storage. John sent the required information and documents to the Department of Veterans Affairs for the records to be released.

Three weeks later, John received a letter from the Department of Veterans Affairs stating his request was denied under certain exemptions. A total of sixty-seven pages were being withheld, but he had the option to appeal and was given a phone number if he had any questions. John immediately called the officer in charge to appeal their decision, explaining to them why he needed the information. The officer instructed John to send her a list of questions he specifically wanted answered, in writing, and she would do her best to answer them.

A week later, John received another letter from the officer in response to his list. He was told that there was no documentation indicating when Richard first learned he had AIDS, and no documentation indicating if Janyce knew Richard had AIDS. Richard said he had a girlfriend who used IV drugs, and there was no mention of a deathbed confession. The officer told John that he should try to retrieve copies of his father's medical records from the hospital where he was first admitted prior to being transferred to the Department of Veterans Affairs.

John did as the officer suggested and telephoned the hospital, but he was told that it was their policy to destroy all patient records after ten years, and they had no medical records relating to his father.

* * *

Kim and John had done everything they could think of to find out what really happened in the early morning hours of September 21, 1984. Everywhere they turned, they seemed to run into a wall. Another case in point would be the evidence CSI collected the night Janyce died. A call was made to APD's Crime Lab section to inquire if they still had the evidence, and if it was ever tested. After checking, it was determined that yes, they still had the evidence in a box--Box #36-- including a syringe with liquid, and, no, it was never tested. Sometime later, Kim inquired through an e-mail to Detective Conner if he could have the evidence tested. He later replied that the evidence was destroyed June 13, 1997. This is a complete contradiction to the first inquiry. When asked who, what, why, or how it was destroyed, no one had any answers.

Janyce's case was unsolved. So why was the evidence destroyed before it was ever tested?

Kim telephoned the Arapahoe County District Attorney's office and spoke with Julie* in the intake department. Kim told her they were looking into the death of Janyce Hansen and were writing a book. She explained to Julie how, back in 1984, Detective Lovato tried to make a case against Richard. She had sent the DA several things pertaining to the case, and she was basically ignored. While still on the phone with Kim, Julie tried to locate any information they might have on Richard by entering his name and social security number into their database. She told Kim nothing relating to Janyce's death was coming up.

Julie gave her the name of the District Attorney in 1984, and told her that he has since retired. However, Julie explained, there was one person by the name of David Johnson* who still worked at the DA's office and he had worked with the former DA back in 1984. Julie said she would have him contact Kim.

A couple of days later, Kim received a call from Julie telling her that she wanted to let Kim know she wasn't ignoring her and had given the message to David. He was in a meeting, and she was texting him, while she and Kim were still on the phone, asking him when he would be available. David texted Julie saying he would try to find the file as soon as he was finished with his meeting, then call her back. After that day, Kim never heard back from anyone at the DA's office.

She later received an e-mail from Detective Conner telling her that David Johnson from the District Attorney's Office contacted him concerning this case, and because the case was never presented for filing, they would have no information on it—and not to expect a return phone call. Detective Conner further stated that he saw no merit in opening up a closed investigation based upon supposition, conjecture, speculation, and feelings. He would need something in the form of physical evidence, but even then, to what end? He also wrote in his e-mail that he wasn't going to question an officer about what he may or may not have written in a report about something that happened twenty-six years ago. Detective Conner ended the e-mail telling Kim that he was not actively involved in any follow up with Janyce's case, and if the family felt this was not a fair assessment, to contact his supervisor.

Dr. Dobersen replied in an e-mail saying that unfortunately, anyone from the Coroner's office who had anything to do with this case was dead, and the coroner's case file left much to be desired, and this was exactly why he didn't run his office the way they did back then. So Kim and John were basically told, without any physical evidence, that Janyce's case would remain unsolved, and her death certificate would not be changed.

* * *

They were devastated that Detective Conner, being a Cold Case Detective, wasn't willing to speak with any of the officers, detectives, chief of police, or other individuals involved in the original investigation, including Patricia.

They were determined that Janyce would receive justice. John took it upon himself to speak with Patricia. He called her to see if she wanted to talk about anything, specifically anything that happened the night his mom died. She must have somehow been forewarned that he was going to call her, because all she could say was, "You're recording me, aren't you? Why are you doing this? What do you hope to gain by digging all this up again? You'd better not write anything bad about my dad, not in any book."

John and Kim didn't have the resources to hire the kind of people who could open doors for them. So they thought maybe they should enlist the help of a psychic. John knew that his mom had always believed in the supernatural, and at times she felt a connection to the spiritual world. Maybe through the help of a psychic, they could get some sort of closure on what happened to her. Ever since the start of writing this book, they had often felt the presence of something supernatural. Unexplainable things had happened, sometimes angelic, sometimes demonic. They always felt it was Janyce pulling for them, or Richard pulling them away.

Kim did some research and found Carrie Schubert, a clairvoyant/psychic consultant, lecturer, teacher, author, medium, and certified hypnotherapist. In her spare time, Carrie volunteered to both national and local authorities to help solve crimes and find missing persons.

Kim and John met with Carrie on April 20, 2010. The only information she had prior to their session was their first names, and that they were looking for answers as to how John's mother died.

The session started, and the first thing Carrie got was a name like Annie. Janyce's nickname was Janny. Carrie said what Janny was showing and telling her.

It is dark where she is, and it feels like she fell and hit the back of her head, or someone hit her.

Carrie sees two males and describes to Kim and John what they look like. She also sees a young woman off in the distance. Now she's saying a name like Ralph an R name. Richard's middle name was Ralph. She sees him over there, like he's somewhere else, and Janyce is thinking of him. She feels the two men have come into her place and are blocking her exit.

She feels like she is in a car. There's something outside the car, something green. She's smelling trying to see if its paint. She is in a garage. She feels like she is in an older car, maybe white with green on it, like it's old-fashioned. The inside feels off-white, like cream color. She sees keys dangling, something gold, a keychain. She wonders why she's in the garage. The two men are mocking or taunting Janny, and she's asking, "What did I do?"

Carrie experiences pain all throughout the session in her head, hand, and chest. "I see the girl again, like she's over there witnessing this. She is feeling panicky. She says what are you doing? Why are you doing that? Then she puts her hands over her mouth."

Back to Janny. She is saying to Kim, "You are so good for him." She wants to go to Kim. She needs to clean something up with her. *She wants you to know she appreciates you. She wants to put her arms around you.*

Going to John, she says she is so sorry. *I love you. I miss you.* She has the keys to something. She wants to give them to Johnny, and then he can put it to rest. *Janny is showing me something. I can't make out what it is. It's like a vase or an urn. I think it's white marble with veining in it.* It sounded as if Carrie was describing Janyce's tombstone and the two white marble urns with veining running through them on either side of it.

The session lasted for about an hour. It was very emotional for Kim and John. Carrie hit on many facts that they could connect to. For instance, Janny showed Carrie the powder blue car Johnny used to own. Kim and John's feelings after the session were that the woman who witnessed everything was definitely Patricia. Carrie described her perfectly. They felt certain that one of the men there was John's brother, Niles. Carrie also described another man, provided specific details, and mentioned a few names that John doesn't want to divulge at this time.

None of this is actual proof of anything, but it helps substantiate what John, Jill, and Kim already believe happened the night Janny died. Kim sent a copy of the transcript to Detective Conner from their recorded session they had with Carrie, which included names and descriptions of possible witnesses. Detective Conner wasn't interested in speaking with Carrie, or even pursuing any possible leads.

Since then, John's feelings toward Patricia have become mixed. He feels compassion, sadness, and hatred towards her. A nationally recognized expert in detecting deception, in both verbal and nonverbal behaviors, was recently briefed about Janny's case, and believes Patricia is suffering from Stockholm Syndrome, which occurs when a victim becomes emotionally attached to the kidnapper, or in Patricia's case, the abuser. Her behavior could have grown from a common survival strategy. She may have become so afraid of her dad that she didn't want to displease him in any way.

* * *

Recently, Katrina Laura Klein Masterson, with the United States Federal Government in Washington, D. C., connected with Kim through social networking. She works for the Alcohol, Tobacco, and Firearms (ATF) managing the crisis and trauma intervention programs. In addition, she is currently on the board of the local Court Appointed Special Advocate Association program (CASA) which focuses on child advocacy and crisis intervention.

After having several conversations, Katrina's knowledge, and her expertise within the system have led us to explore new avenues. She spoke with an F.B.I. agent in Washington about our suspicions. In turn, the F.B.I. agent referred the case to a Special Agent with the F.B.I. in Denver. The Special Agent looked into the case and agreed--if there were ties to the mafia--she would pursue it. If not, she would turn it over to the Colorado Attorney General's Office, because it would be out of the F.B.I's jurisdiction. She would begin by calling former Detective Lovato.

During the same time period, Kim made contact with the now retired CSI Agent McGoff, the same agent who processed the scene and took the photos on the evening in question. As everyone else we contacted, he remembered it well. He suggested they meet over a cup of coffee at a restaurant (public place) near him to discuss the case. He also suggested everyone bring someone along for safety sake. Since John and Kim lived several hundred miles away from McGoff, they all agreed they would communicate with each other by phone and e-mails.

Following is a statement McGoff provided in an e-mail to John and Kim.

"I remember the case… As to my belief, there was corruption … both Sergeant Davis and I had problems with the story Richard told. We had problems with the lack of coloring on the victim from the carbon monoxide…she never showed signs while still at the scene. That bothered us both. The fact the car was not running, lights on. Richard's report of having to go back for his coat at the time that the restaurant's/bars would be closing. His or someone's belt in the car. And her purse upstairs in the bathroom."

McGoff also told John and Kim when he arrived on scene that night the garage doors were closed (as evidenced in the crime scene photos), and no smell of exhaust.

He went on to write, "As for any corruption in Aurora, a Division Chief once announced in a meeting with his division, 'Does corruption exist in Aurora, sure it does.' Came as no shock to me... I tried for several years to get investigations going on activities within the Aurora PD. From City Hall to the Arapahoe County DA I never found anyone I could trust. At one point, I had a deputy DA tell me that everything I was reporting to the DA was being reported right back to the PD. From there I never found anyone to trust. I even received a warning from an investigator that I and my family could be in danger if I continued. I transferred to the gang unit where I remained until near the end of my career. I have no reason to believe that any of that has changed except perhaps some names. ...You might be better off contacting someone away from the metro area actually. Some of the names contained in your e-mails and this investigation have come up in the past."

In a telephone conversation with John and Kim, McGoff tells them if they can arrange a meeting with someone whom they have been speaking with, either with the F.B.I. or Attorney General's Office--who has the authority to launch an internal investigation--he would agree to sit down face-to-face with them. He also would be willing to speak with Dr. Dobersen about the case, but would not divulge to him specific names or information pertaining to the corruption.

Finally, things were starting to go John and Kim's way. Here was someone who had worked for the Aurora Police Department and had information that he would only be willing to share with a select few individuals. Facts, not only pertaining to this case, but information that something was (probably still is) seriously wrong with the Aurora Police Department. Kim contacts Dr. Dobersen and the F.B.I Special Agent with this new information and requests they both speak with McGoff.

In the meantime, Kim and John are both invited to speak on an internet radio talk show "Crime Wire Investigates". The Crime Wire team is a network of private and forensic investigators and legal experts who have come together to help families seek justice for their loved ones. After reviewing Janny's case, the team believes her death is a clear-cut case of murder. Dr. Dobersen is invited to call into the show. He accepts. Susan Murphy-Milano, one of the members and hosts of Crime Wire, feels that he is their greatest strength in bringing justice to Janny.

So, now, we have renewed hope. The Aurora Police Department, Colorado Attorney General's Office, F.B.I, Arapahoe County District

Attorney's Office, and the Arapahoe County Coroner are all involved. They are all aware that we want justice for Janny, and the only way that can be obtained is if her death certificate is changed from "undetermined" to "homicide". Dr. Dobersen is the only person with the authority to change it.

Our renewed hope is short lived when, once again, Kim contacts the authorities for updates. She finds out that no one has tried to contact McGoff, and every agency involved turned the case back over to the Arapahoe County Coroner's Office and the Aurora Police Department--reasoning there is not enough compelling evidence to see this as a homicide.

Still upset with Dr. Dobersen for not calling into the Crime Wire show, Kim writes an e-mail to him. It seems he had a prior engagement and was unavailable. She asks when the death certificate will be changed to "homicide". He replies that he can find no evidence to rule Janyce's death a homicide, but offers two suggestions. Since no one has contacted McGoff or Lovato, he would be willing to speak with them, and offers to perform an autopsy on Janyce's remains--if the family pays $4,000 for the disinterment/re-interment.

A couple days later, Kim receives an e-mail from McGoff telling her Dr. Dobersen called him and writes "My discussion with Dr. Dobersen left me with the impression he wants a resolution to this that is based on all possible information. The lack of an autopsy and the Jewish burial without embalming presents severe problems to overcoming/overturning the original determination. Any evidence of wrong doing could be gone now. Although there have been cases where the remains did present evidence...but please don't take that as an indication/promise that that would happen with this case. I expressed my doubts on Mr. Hansen's statements and expressed my reasons why. I also expressed my opinion on the investigation, and the abrupt end of the investigation, as well as actions of the coroner's office…"

Kim e-mails Dr. Dobersen again requesting an update. He replies stating he did speak with both McGoff and Lovato and the bottom line is that, while expressing misgivings and dissatisfaction with the Aurora PD and the Coroner's Office (at that time) on a number of issues, they could offer no evidence that Janyce's death was a homicide.

Whether or not Dr. Dobersen senses her hostility in the emails, Kim is not happy with the responding email she receives from him. He writes "If you think that anyone in this investigation, either in 1984 or the present, has a reason to or has covered up anything, we would all like to hear some concrete facts not just the ramblings of individuals with bad feelings and grievances about their former employers." He states that he agrees an autopsy should have been done and his offer still stands to do one now on the remains--if the family pays the $4,000.00 for disinterment/re-interment.

After reflecting back on everything that has transpired over the past two years, and the fact their mother had a Jewish burial, John and Jill have decided not to move forward. Recalling the words former Agent McGoff wrote to them in one of his last e-mails--"Spent years trying to correct the uncorrectable in the APD...left with my soul intact, to save my family and myself further grief."--John and Jill have chosen to do the same.

* * *

The twenty eight months spent researching and writing this book has come to an end. So many people opened their doors to us, only to close them after corresponding through several phone calls and e-mails. We've concluded that people aren't talking to us, because either they are afraid, or feel they don't have to. It seems that the authorities are taking the path of least resistance, and we can't force them into doing what we think they should do. John and Jill believe that if a thorough investigation would have been done, the outcome would be much different.

Now, they are left with the haunting question they so desperately need answered. Will their mother, Janyce Hansen, ever receive justice? They hope to someday have complete closure, but feel that can only come through discovering the truth about what really happened on the night of September 20, 1984, and early morning hours of September 21, 1984. They feel that Patricia holds the key to everything. If she would only tell them, or the authorities, what happened that night, they could finally have closure, and their mother would have the justice she deserves after all these years.

* * *

John and Jill are making a personal plea to anyone who has any information about their mother's death and her unsolved case to please come forward and contact them through info at jaksgoldenknights dot com

AFTERWORD

John and Jill have gained a certain amount of closure through the writing of this book. Just making their lives public, in and of itself, was a major hurdle for them to cross. Jill came close to actually paying with her life for trying to free herself from her painful memories.

In 2006, she was diagnosed with Cushing's Syndrome. Given the fact that the disease is rarely diagnosed, the doctors felt that she may have been suffering with it for many years. Jill underwent two separate surgeries, and due to complications, she is still very sick, and is forced to take large doses of steroids. She takes one day at a time and gets most of her happiness from her children and friends, and has a close relationship with her brother, John, his wife, Kim, and their two children.

Both of Jill's sons, Travis and Gavin, live in Colorado in the Denver metro area, and are both enrolled in college. Travis plans to become a corporate attorney, and Gavin an architectural engineer. Kelsi still lives with her dad in Denver and visits Jill on the weekends. She is a junior in high school, a straight-A student, and is an exceptional soccer and volleyball player.

On July 13, 2011, John celebrated fourteen years of sobriety. On November 5 of this year, he and Kim will celebrate twenty-three years of marriage. Earlier this year, Kim was diagnosed with an extremely rare form of cancer and underwent surgery to remove it. In the months that followed, she had another biopsy, which was benign. She remains cancer free and has returned to work as a paralegal with a Phoenix law firm, and plans to become a licensed Private Investigator. Their daughter is a sophomore in high school and Honor Roll student. Their son is in eighth grade, a straight A-student, member of the National Junior Honor Society, and plays on the school's soccer team.

John continues to work in telecommunications as a Regional Markets Representative and has won several awards, including President's Circle, and manages to stay consistently in the top ten as a sales representative throughout the country. He enjoys playing golf and is a member of a local golf league. John has tried to put the bad memories behind him and to remember only the good. His plans are to become a professional speaker/victim's advocate against child abuse and domestic violence, in his spare time.

On March 7, 2010, Janyce's mother and John's and Jill's grandmother, Molly Cohen Bloom, died at the age of 101 at the retirement home in Scottsdale, Arizona. Her body was flown back to Denver, Colorado, and laid to rest in Rose Hill Cemetery beside her husband, Ben, the same cemetery where Janny is buried.

ABOUT THE AUTHOR

Photo by Shellani Jensen

SHERRIE LUEDER was born on November 13, 1951 in Tracy, Minnesota and christened Sherrie Rae Taarud. She would be the second oldest of four siblings. She met her husband, a lifelong resident of Wisconsin, where they chose to settle and raise their four children.

Sherrie loved spending her summers near the water and enjoyed long days of lounging on the beach reading mystery novels and writing poetry. One of her poems *"A Tribute to Mom"* was published in a local newspaper (The Lake Park News, December 29, 1979), and later in *Eddie-Lou Cole's Anthology of Great Poems*. She continues to write poetry, and is currently working on her second book.

Made in the USA
Charleston, SC
23 September 2011